Fresh Oil From Heaven

Fresh Oil From Heaven

Ed Dufresne

Ed Dufresne Ministries
P.O. Box 186
Temecula, CA 92593

Unless otherwise indicated,
all scriptural quotations are taken from
the *King James Version* of the Bible.

Fresh Oil From Heaven
ISBN 0-940763-00-2
Copyright © 1987 by
Ed Dufresne Ministries
P.O. Box 186
Temecula, CA 92593

Third Printing, December 1992

Published by
Ed Dufresne Publications
P.O. Box 186
Temecula, CA 92593

Contents

Foreword

Foreword

For a number of years I have personally known Ed Dufresne. I first knew him as a pastor in California. Later I came to know him as an evangelist and teacher of the Word of God.

I deeply appreciate Ed Dufresne's humility before the Lord; and his compassion for lost souls and for sick and suffering humanity is exciting to me.

This new volume, *Fresh Oil From Heaven*, is a message for this hour. God is giving the fresh oil of the Holy Ghost. There is revival on planet earth. The oil is flowing and God is moving.

May the contents of this book both inspire you and challenge you. These are the last days and Jesus is coming soon. Let us labor for the Master, "for in such an hour as you think not, the Son of Man cometh."

Lester Sumrall

Fresh Oil From Heaven

Chapter 1
Fresh Oil From Heaven

The Bible says that God will show His children things to come (John 16:13); and before God does anything on this earth, He'll show it to His prophets: *Surely the Lord God will do nothing, but he revealeth his secret unto his servants the prophets* (Amos 3:7). Then the prophets, as the Spirit wills, are to speak out what is about to happen.

The year 1987 marked the beginning of the next great move of God. I believe this with every fiber of my being.

I got saved in 1966, and the day I got saved is the day I began working in the ministry, although I began in the ministry of helps. (The ministry of helps, whether you know it or not, is found in First Corinthians 12:28.)

The day I got saved is the day I went to the pastor and told him, "I must be involved. My heart is burning with love for God, and I want to work for Him." And from that day forward, I've been busy for God.

This is my 20th year of ministry. In the Word of God, 20 is an important number. You'll find that some very important things happened in 20-year intervals.

I don't know what's in your heart right now, but I know about mine: I am hungry for the perfect will of God in my life. I don't want to miss it; I don't want to miss this wave of God.

God's Times of Refreshing

Let's look at Acts 3:19:

Repent ye therefore, and be converted, that your

1

sins may be blotted out, when the times of refreshing shall come from the presence of the Lord.

Acts 3:19

What does it say? *Repent!* I don't know about you, but I've been doing a lot of repenting during the last three years. It seems that every time I turn around, the Holy Spirit is dealing with my attitude. And I believe that's what God has been doing to the Church in the last three years. I've made the decision that I'm going to repent of my ways.

Now notice the word "times" in this verse. "Times" means time is measured by numbers, and it's by the clock. "Times" means there are specific times in God's plans, such as "times of refreshing." Did you know that the Church has times of refreshing? God just showed that to me. I believe 1987 was the beginning of a time of refreshing from God: *...when the times of refreshing shall come from the presence of God.*

Right now the Church needs a visitation from God! People are running all over the country looking for methods and formulas to make their church or ministry grow. They're looking to men's plans.

They need to get on their knees, find out what God's plan is, get the fresh oil of anointing from God, and then do the plan that God has given them.

When a refreshing comes from the presence of God, the Holy Spirit starts moving, people are drawn to the meetings, and they don't even want to leave afterwards, because the power of God is so strong. *This time of refreshing — with its miracles — is starting to happen all over this nation.* It's coming from the presence of the Lord!

Another translation of Acts 3:19 reads, "And when the times of *recovery of breath* come from the presence of the Lord...." *Recovery of breath!* The Church needs a recovery of breath!

2

Seasons of refreshing have been experienced throughout the history of the Church. Lately, God's been dealing with me along this line, and I've been studying about revivals and waves of God in the past.

How many of you know what happened in 1907? The Azusa Street Revival broke out then. Actually, it broke out a little earlier in Topeka, Kansas, and other places, but the wave really got going in 1907. That's when it started spreading across the nation and around the world.

The Assemblies of God denomination came out of that 1907 revival. The Pentecostal Holiness denomination also came out of that move. However, that move of God started waning in 1944, 1945, and 1946.

The Importance of 40-Year Cycles

Then came 1947 (the year Smith Wigglesworth died) — 40 years after Azusa Street. As I studied, *I found that a recovery of breath has come to the Church every 40 years!*

One reason we need these times of refreshing is because after a wave hits and everyone has been floating on that wave for a while, they don't want to get on the new wave when it comes along.

When the Holy Spirit starts doing something else, they say, "No, this is the way we've been doing it, and we're going to keep doing it this way," and they ride that old wave all the way in to the beach. Then they start pitching their little tents there. It always has happened that way.

During the fiery Methodist movement, when there was such a flow of the Holy Ghost, people spoke in tongues. Now you can hardly find a Methodist church where the people speak in tongues. You can hardly find a Methodist church where they preach the Word. They read out of *Reader's Digest*.

I'd say that 80 percent of the denominations that came out of the 1907 revival are dead. Why? Because they wouldn't move with the Holy Ghost. They wouldn't move with the plan of God.

Then, in 1947, a healing revival hit planet Earth! It originated in the United States. This is the revival Oral Roberts, Kenneth E. Hagin, and T. L. Osborn came out of. At the end of World War II, God spoke to Brother Hagin and told him a wave of healing would soon spread across this nation, so Brother Hagin got ready for it.

One thing I learned from Brother Hagin, Lester Sumrall, Brother Roberts and Brother Osborn is to flow with *every* move of God that comes along. They flow with each move and prosper from it. They don't get their "surfboards" out and ride back on the old wave with their gift. They don't join the crowd that's up on the beach, saying, "We did this in 1907, and this is the way it's going to be forever!" (That's the attitude that causes your church to dry up.)

My brother and sister, you've got to be on the edge of the new wave. That's what I'm praying for. I don't want to miss God in this next wave. I want to be in the right position — in God's perfect will — to be in this next move of God.

When the 1947 wave came, the 1907 people said, "That ain't of God! They're fanatics!" And what happened? The people riding the new wave had to go out of the churches and hold their healing meetings in tents. (Even many of the Full Gospel people who came out of the 1907 wave didn't want to flow with the new wave of God that started in 1947.)

Even so, revival broke out. Healings took place. God raised up healing ministries to go to the nations. Many of these men and women of God are not alive today, and that's really tragic. Among the few who are left are Brother Hagin, Brother Roberts, Brother Sumrall, and T. L. Osborn.

I don't believe it was the perfect plan of God for the healing meetings to be held in tents, but they had to do it because of the people who had camped up on the beach, saying, "God can only move like He did in 1907. And that's the way it is." No, God can't be placed in a box.

Don't Miss the Wave!

The denominations that came out of the 1907 wave missed the 1947 wave; they missed the 1967 wave — and they'll probably miss the wave that started in 1987! I don't know about you, but I am determined to be in the middle of what God is doing on planet Earth!

I don't know exactly what happened in 1927. But I got something out of my spirit (not my head), that Brother Wigglesworth, Aimee Semple McPherson, and John G. Lake did some important things for God beginning in that time period.

When the tide starts getting low, every 20 years there's a shot in the arm to restore it. Let's look at the year 1967, which is 20 years after the 1947 healing wave started.

In 1967 in Buffalo, New York, Brother Hagin became very ill. He prayed, "God, what is the problem?" And the Lord replied, "You haven't obeyed Me. You haven't done what I told you to do. I'm going to heal you, but I want you to go back to Tulsa and start holding seminars." The Lord told Brother Hagin to teach on faith and prayer in those seminars.

And do you know who came out of those meetings? Ministers like Vicki Jamison-Peterson, Kenneth Copeland, and others. Out of that 1967 meeting, another great wave of God started. It gained so much strength that it took us all the way through 1986. And what do we call it? The Word of Faith Movement.

It's been 20 years now that we've been preaching the Word of Faith. It came out of the Charismatic Wave. Did you know there are people who are still trying to ride the Charismatic Wave — even though that wave was beached 20 years ago?

We saw that there were people in the 1907 wave who didn't want to go with the 1947 wave. And many from both of those waves didn't want to go with the Charismatic Wave — and they certainly didn't want to go with the Word of Faith Wave. But that's why their churches are becoming dead.

There's an alarm going off in my spirit. I say this with love in my heart, but *I am afraid that many churches are going to miss the next wave of God.*

God's been dealing with us. Something is happening. That past wave is pulling back—and *we're about ready for a tidal wave!* As we saw earlier, every 20 years there's a shot in the arm where the tide comes up—but every 40 years, the big waves come. 1907 to 1947 is how many years? *Forty!* From 1947 to 1987 is how many years? *Forty!*

I believe there's a timetable that God goes by. If you study the history of the Church, you'll find that important moves of God have taken place every 20 and 40 years. And we're due for the tidal wave!

I don't know about you, but I'm ready for a refreshing breath from heaven. This country is ready too. We in the United States have heard the best evangelists; we've had the best teachers — but they have only taken us to a certain point. The Body of Christ has been fed, but we haven't moved the sinners.

Yes, some have been saved; don't misunderstand me. Some were saved during the Charismatic Movement too. Praise God for Demos Shakarian and his colleagues in the Full Gospel Business Men's Fellowship. But that wave has waned, and now we must get before God and find out what He wants, and how He wants us to flow.

When 1987 rolled around, something came upon me, giving me the desire to want to go another 40 years for God, if Jesus tarries. I've already worked for Him for 20 years, but now I want to go another 40.

Anointed With Fresh Oil!

Let's look at Psalm 92:10: *But my horn shalt thou exalt like the horn of an unicorn: I shall be anointed with fresh oil.*

The Church needs fresh oil! Christians need a recovery of breath, because the tide just went way down. Have you ever been hit so hard the breath was knocked out of you? I believe that's the condition of the Church right now. I've been at this for 20 years, and I'd certainly like another breath.

I remember an old, '39 Mercury convertible I had. It was lavender, and it had red flames painted on the front of it. Its white roof was "chopped," meaning it was cut in half.

A '39 Mercury had the old floor shift on it. I owned the leakiest piece of machinery there ever was. There was no oil in the rear end, and there was no oil in the transmission, because it would always leak out, so you'd hear it whine. How many have heard the rear end of a car with no oil? The noise would drive you crazy! And then when you changed gears (and there's no oil in the transmission box), it would make another terrible sound.

Don't laugh: That's the way the Church is right now! I go in churches and hear them whining. "The pastor did this; and Brother So-and-so did that; and the pastor's wife got a new dress..." All you hear is whining and complaining, because all the oil has leaked out. You've got to put some oil in your transmission, or you're going to blow it up!

Miracles Without Oil

And *people are trying to have miracle services with no oil.* They're trying to do it intellectually. But there's no oil in your transmission, honey. You can't get out of first gear and get in second.

7

Are you listening to me? Are you hearing what the Spirit of God is saying?

The Church needs some fresh oil from heaven!

It's gotten so bad that if somebody gets up and speaks in tongues—even in a Full Gospel church—they haul them out the back door. They don't want the Holy Ghost in their services!

If a person who needed to be raised from the dead was brought into some of our churches today, the people would pass out. If you told them he'd been dead for three days, you'd hear a loud noise from the people, and the pastor would whine, "O God, I've got to change gears!"

Instead, we ought to be able to go to services that are charged with the anointing of the Holy Spirit, and when the preacher gets up to speak, you don't hear any whining.

When the pastor announces, "Now, everybody come out for prayer meeting on Tuesday night," we shouldn't hear the whiners say: "I've got work to do at home." "You know I'm busy." "We've got responsibilities."

And when they all begin dancing and praising God, they shouldn't brag, "Oh, we're in the *Spirit!*" when they're actually in the *flesh.* (I'll have more to say on the subject of dancing later.) They shouldn't claim, "We're bringing the Spirit of God into the service" when they're really pushing Him out by grieving Him!

Furthermore, Sister Bucketmouth shouldn't go to the piano and announce, "I've got a song from the Lord" — and all you hear is banging, clanging, and grinding of gears because of no oil.

That's the way the Church is. We're clanging. We're talking faith words, but we're clanging and whining — and what we need is a revival of fresh oil from heaven.

Someone may ask, "Why are you picking on the Church?" Well, the Church is my family, and I want my family to do the will of God. I don't want anyone in the Body of Christ to miss this next wave.

What happens when we get this fresh oil from heaven mentioned in Psalm 92? Verse 11 goes on to tell us, *Mine eye also shall see my desire on mine enemies, and mine ears shall hear my desire of the wicked that rise up against me.*

I know preachers who have fought every devil in hell in recent years. Actually, the last four years have been rather tough for this preacher too. We preachers are still here, but we could use some fresh oil after 20 years of labor and work.

The Church needs fresh oil from heaven!

The Church needs oil from heaven to fight the devil!

Will the Church Go With the Wave?

I'm ready for '87 and the years to follow! I'm turned on to the Word of God! I just hope that those of us who go with this next wave don't have to go outside the Church. It grieves me when pastors get so upset about their little formalities, and they won't allow the gifts of the Spirit to operate, because they get scared.

It won't be God's first choice to have this move take place outside the Church. We have seen that those in the Healing Wave, the Charismatic Wave, and the Faith Wave all had to go out of the Church. In the Word of Faith Movement, God raised up a whole new breed of churches, because so many Full Gospel/Pentecostal churches wouldn't allow faith to be preached in them.

The Lord has been saying to me, "If I have to, I'll raise up a whole new breed of Holy Ghost churches that *will* allow the Word of God and the Holy Ghost to flow."

Don't misunderstand me: There were some in the 1907 group who went with the healing group, and those churches are flourishing today, because they went with every wave of God.

9

I don't know about you, but I'm going to flow in the Holy Ghost wave. I'm getting my spiritual surfboard all waxed up, and I'm going to ride that wave in, glory be to God!

False Doctrines and Old Doctrines

Every time a wave is about ready to take off, the devil comes in and sows a lot of false doctrine. It started in 1985, and you're seeing all kinds of doctrines in the Church today.

One doctrine does away with the Rapture, even though that's one of the fundamental doctrines of the Bible. (What hope do you have if there's no Rapture?)

And then there's a group that's arguing about the spirit and the soul: Are they one, or are they divided? I could care less.

I want you to know that I'm going to preach Jesus and Him crucified. You can argue all you want about your old doctrines, and this deep "revy" (revelation) and that deep "revy." The "revy" seekers run to and fro — and one of these days they're going to run right off a cliff!

But I'm going to stay with the Word of God. Why? Because the Church hasn't even grasped Mark 11:23-25 yet. I'm going to ignore these doctrinal arguments. I don't think that way. Do you know how I think? I ask myself: Does that doctrine get anyone healed? Does it get anyone delivered? Does it set anyone free? Does it reach people in my neighborhood or my community? (If not, it's not worth a thing!)

Churches today are full of sick people. I would say that 85 percent of the congregation comes forward for healing in my services—and we've been teaching healing for 20 years! (Where's their oil?)

Other scratchy sounds are heard from that other bunch, the "hyper-revy church." That church is tossed around by every revelation that comes along. (You need some oil in your transmission, honey.)

If we're going to supersede the Book of Acts, we shouldn't call it The Acts of the Apostles; we should call it "The Acts of the Holy Ghost," because that's what it is: the acts of the Holy Ghost flowing through the New Testament Church.

Fresh oil flowed on the Day of Pentecost. Fresh oil flowed into Peter and John, who were immediately transformed and began to do exploits for God, such as healing the lame man at the Gate Beautiful.

A New Beginning

It just didn't seem like I ever fitted into the teaching wave, even though I taught the Word of God. I had some good tapes too. But God told me to burn all my teaching tapes three years ago. I had about 40,000 names on my mailing list, and He said, "Burn your mailing list. Those methods worked then, but now you're going to start with a fresh breath from heaven."

That doesn't mean we're to do away with the teaching of the Word, because the Word always works. It just means we're to be aware of new directions the new wave may be taking us.

This may be the last wave of God. Maybe Jesus is coming during the next 20 years. I don't know. But many people believe He's coming around the year 2000. Dr. Sumrall has studied the numbers that seem to be on God's timetable, and he says it looks like Jesus could come around 2000 — but he's not predicting it; he's just sharing that information.

I don't know when Jesus is returning. He may come tomorrow. I doubt it, however, *because we haven't outdone the Book of Acts yet.* I haven't heard of too many people walking by city hall and raising up a crippled man, as Peter and John did. I haven't seen a preacher stand up in one of my meetings and disappear, only to show up in another part of the country, as Philip did.

If this is the last wave, I believe that *all the waves from the Day of Pentecost to 1987 will combine to hit planet Earth!*

It's Time for Fresh Oil

Fresh oil will flow from heaven. When the oil flows, there will be those who will come out of wheelchairs. Oil from heaven will flow into deaf ears and they will hear. Oil from heaven will flow into blind eyes and they will see.

Times of refreshing came in '47 and '67 — and the oil started flowing again in '87, which was the beginning of another time of refreshing. It's time for fresh oil from heaven!

What started to happen in '87? Miracles. Fresh oil. *There's going to be another healing revival, but mostly there will be miracles, signs, and wonders that the world hasn't seen before.*

The gifts of the Spirit will be in operation. There will be some who won't go with it, but there will be other churches that will be raised up, and they'll have Holy Ghost church services. But no man will get the credit for this wave, because it will be a wave of the Holy Ghost.

Flow with the Holy Ghost and you will prosper. Flow with the Holy Ghost, and the gifts of the Spirit will operate, and you will not be cheated at the game of life. You'll be on top of things when you flow with the Holy Ghost.

Lord, we need fresh oil from heaven!

Chapter 2
Recovery of Breath

For some time, the Lord has been dealing with me about "recovery of breath." "The Church needs a recovery of breath," the Lord said.

We need some old-time religion! The Church is dead. People don't even shout anymore in some churches. If you've got joy and victory in your heart, you're going to want to shout about it. Their excuse in these dead churches is, "Well, you know, brother, I'm just kind of low key. I'm *sedate.*"

Yes, and you're dead too! Because God has given you something to shout about. (If your favorite football team makes a touchdown, you get excited about it, don't you?)

The Church needs a second breath of old-time religion and the resurrection power of God. I'm excited. I think some old-time religion got on me. (I'm from California, where we aren't so dignified.) Praise the Lord for the refreshing from heaven; a second breath from heaven.

What happened in 1907 isn't going to work in 1987. We need a refreshing breath. We need the power of the Living God to come into our churches so much that the newscasters will visit and report, "Oh, there's action going on down there in that church. Things are happening. People are coming into the church in wheelchairs, and they're walking out pushing them. The man who was crippled is now pushing the preacher around in the wheelchair!"

I'm not trying to be anyone else but me. I'm praying for God's will in my life; not my will. He has told me, "In 1987,

13

you will start going across the land with some old-time resurrection power in your ministry."

"Now, brother, I'm not for all that yelling," some people tell me. I answer, "Just wait a while. You're liable to get picked up out of that chair of yours, get lifted up in mid-air, and have the power of God shake you and throw you back down. You're liable to get your suit all dirty and wrinkled in the process, glory to God! But you'll come up shouting and praying in the Holy Ghost!

Resurrection Power

I believe in this next wave we're going to get fresh revelation from heaven about the resurrection power — the power that raised Jesus from the dead. Our preachers need to be resurrected with the power of the Living God.

One reason we don't have any resurrection power is because we've eliminated our prayer time. Now people say, "Well, you only need to pray once, and that's it." They don't pray anymore. They'd rather watch television than get on their knees and intercede before God!

They'd rather have everyone's tapes all lined up so they can just push a button and instantly get the tape they need. They talk about someone else's experiences. But I want my own experience with the Holy Ghost! I don't want to just talk about Smith Wigglesworth's experiences of raising people from the dead; I want the same experiences in my life! I don't want to just hear about what happened in Maria Woodworth-Etter's ministry; I want what happened in her ministry to happen in *my* ministry.

And I want it in every church. Happy Caldwell says, "You never know what Ed Dufresne is going to do." It's because you never know what the Holy Ghost is going to do. But I'd rather have the reputation of being a Holy Ghost man than to be a dry, predictable preacher.

In one church, the power of God came on me while I was drinking some water from a glass, and the Lord said, "Go to that section over there, and throw that water on them. Everyone it hits will be healed." So I just threw the water on them. People screamed as they were being healed. Some people's legs were straightened out by the power of God.

I went back to that church to hold a meeting, and when I picked up a glass of water to take a drink, the place came unglued. They thought I was going to do it again! But it won't work everytime just because the Holy Ghost had me do it once. Just because Jesus spit once and someone was healed doesn't mean you should spit on people. If you spit on some man's wife and it doesn't work, you're in trouble, buddy! But if you're under the unction of the Holy Ghost and He tells you to do it, it's a different story.

Walking in the Holy Ghost is an adventurous life! I can't wait to get to my meetings to see what the Holy Ghost is going to do!

Sitting by the Fire

Do you know what a lot of preachers remind me of? Peter. How many remember when the Lord told Peter, "You're going to deny me three times?"

Peter was waiting around to see what was going to happen to Jesus when a young woman came up to him and asked, "Aren't you the fellow who was with Jesus?"

When a woman can talk a preacher out of his anointing, something is wrong. It's not that women are bad, but more preachers have fallen because of women than anything else. Women are one of the major "tools" the devil uses to get men to quit preaching the Word or to get them luke-warm.

So she said to Peter, "Aren't you the fellow who was with Jesus? Aren't you the fellow who was over there preaching the Word of God with that fellow Jesus? Wasn't that you with Him?"

"Oh, no. Not me."

Peter had been sitting by a fire that had been built in the hall of the High Priest's house, but after the servant woman asked him those questions, Peter began retreating.

That's the trouble with a lot of preachers: They're backing up! They're backing away from the Word of God. They're all sitting around a nice little fire, thinking, "Well, I don't know...I don't like persecution. I think I'll just find a nice doctrine that's floating around — a doctrine everyone will receive."

They're also thinking, "I want to *submit* to somebody. I'll submit to a denomination within the Full Gospel people. I'm just tired of fighting. I want somebody else to pray for me and do my fighting for me. Oh, this is so nice and warm!

And someone comes walking by and asks, "Aren't you the fellow who was preaching that Word of Faith stuff?"

"Oh, no. Not me."

"Aren't you the name-it-and-claim-it guy? You were over there with that other name-it-and-claim-it guy, Jesus — the One who said you can have what you say."

"Oh, no. Not me! Oh, it feels just right here. It's nice and warm. I don't have to be in that cold jail anymore."

You know this is true. You know they're backing off. A lot of preachers have lost their fire. And I'll tell you another thing they've done: They don't have any more pioneer spirit. Instead, they want to *submit, submit.* Yes, we need to submit to one another—don't misunderstand me. But they want to submit to someone *because they're tired of fighting.* They're laying down their weapons. They've got their eyes on their secretary!

That's what happens, honey, when you get by the fire, start warming up, and watch X-rated movies. Before you know it, you're backing up and saying, "Oh, no. I'm not with that bunch anymore; I'm with another bunch." It's easy to walk that way, compromising in everything.

Many preachers excuse themselves by saying, "Well, you know we've got a new building now." I go to some churches and the pastors brag, "We have several millionaires and doctors in our church." Big deal! I don't care if they're *all* wearing Rolex watches. That doesn't impress me a bit.

"Look at our building. Look at what God has done for us."

"Do you preach faith anymore?"

"Oh, no. Not me. I got with this bunch that's keeping everything of mine nice and warm."

Then another fellow comes by, and says a third time. "I know you. You're one of those guys who believes in speaking in tongues, casting out devils, and praying for the sick."

"Oh, no. Not me. You know, there's something else that's popular now. It's called *unbelief*."

It's possible for a preacher to put his gear box in neutral, get all his orders from headquarters, and now he doesn't have to get on his knees and pray anymore.

Peter denied Jesus, and then the rooster crowed. I want you to know, the "rooster" already has crowed, and they're dropping like flies. They're denying the resurrection power! They're denying the doctrine of healing! They're *even* denying tongues! I mean it! They're preaching that you shouldn't pray in tongues anymore because you need to understand your prayers with your mind. They've gotten into a head trip. But we can't figure the things of God out in our head!

Now, I praise God for teachers, but I have a problem with those who "Greek" everything out. They'll start with a *lemon tree*, for example. Then they'll get the root word over here, the root word over there, and the root word over there—and before you know it, they've got a *plum tree!* And do you want to know why? It's because they've got a *plum tree doctrine*, and they want to prove it's right.

But something happened to wimpy Peter. A wave of God came. Oil came. That's going to happen to some of the dead preachers too. They're going to get this book and call me. They'll ask, "What's wrong with you?"

I'll say, "You backslidden preacher — get away from the fire! Get away from that woman who isn't your wife! Get away from that unbelief you've been preaching! Get some oil in your life and stand up and fight! Quit being a wimp!"

If what you're preaching isn't in line with the Word of God, it is nothing but hot air — clanging gears. Some preachers just want to promote their little pet doctrine across the nation. Sitting by the fire was popular in Jesus' day too. Being *with* Jesus certainly wasn't. And it's the same today. We've come full circle. At one time it was popular to preach faith. It's getting to where it isn't anymore.

Peter had become a backslidden preacher. He had denied his Lord. He needed some fresh oil from heaven to get him fired up again. The Lord told me that's where a lot of preachers are.

What do you tell people when they ask you what church you go to? What do you tell them when they ask, "What does your church believe?"

If you say, "We believe in casting out devils," they may say, "Oh, you're one of those who will hook up with Jesus."

"Yes, I'm one of those fellows. I'm a Jesus fellow, or I'm a Jesus woman." That's what you women ought to be: Jesus women. Don't mess around with the devil or any of his friends. The devil won't want to mess with you when you use the Name of Jesus on him. Run him off your husband! Run that alcohol devil off him! Quit complaining. Get up and walk away from the fire where you talk self-pity: "Oh, poor me. Poor me."

Get out of there; get in the Word of God; and become a Jesus woman, or a Jesus man.

Men, stand up and don't allow the devil to get in your "garden." That's what happened to Adam. He's the one who got us into this mess! I'm going to have to face Adam when I get to heaven for saying that, but it's the truth. It wasn't the woman who committed high treason; it was the man. The man should have run the devil out of his garden, but he was sitting over by the fire.

He was saying, "Come on, honey. Let's sin together. You know, if we watch X-rated movies, it will help our sex life. It will help us."

No it won't. It will damn your soul. It will allow evil spirits to come into your home through your television set.

I hope this goes all over the nation so those backslidden preachers will quit sitting around their fires of denomination and quitting.

We need to *refire*. We need to take what we learned in the last twenty years and go on with this next wave.

We're not supposed to relax on what we have learned. We're supposed to take it and use it on the devil!

Now we'll get back to Peter. Something happened to him in his backslidden state.

They'd Been With Jesus

Now when Jesus was risen early the first day of the week, he appeared first to Mary Magdalene, out of whom he had cast seven devils.

And she went and told them that had been with him, as they mourned and wept.

And they, when they had heard that he was alive, and had been seen of her, believed not.

After that he appeared in another form unto two of them, as they walked, and went into the country.

And they went and told it unto the residue: neither believed they them.

Afterward he appeared unto the eleven as they sat

at meat, and upbraided them with their unbelief and hardness of heart, because they believed not them which had seen him after he was risen.

Mark 16:9-14

And when Jesus was risen. . . . Praise God, He is risen! I'm not serving a dead Jesus. Buddha is dead; there's no power in him.

. . . He appeared first to Mary Magdalene, out of whom he had cast seven devils. A person who has been delivered from seven devils is going to love you! There are people running around in your city who are full of devils, and if you can get them set free, they'll love you. They'll come to your aid when you need help.

And she [Mary] *went and told them that had been with him* [that she had seen Jesus], *as they mourned and wept.* Mary went to see Jesus' disciples. How would you like to have a staff like this? They were crying. They thought Jesus was dead. Too many Christians today think Jesus is dead too. Every time they receive Communion, they do it "in memory" of Him. But the Bible doesn't say to take Communion "in memory" of a dead Jesus; it says to put yourself "in remembrance" of what happened at Calvary.

How many have been in a graveyard where the tombstones say, "In memory of So-and-so." That means the person is dead. But Jesus is not dead. He rose on the third day. He's alive and doing well.

But a bunch of preachers today are denying the resurrection power. They would rather listen to some "seduction" book. I'll tell you, if you read it, it will "seduce" you all right — right into unbelief. It talks away the gifts of the Spirit. It also refers to some great heroes of faith as devils. Actually, these men were mightily used by God. You don't call Dr. Paul Yonggi Cho a devil!

Men who write books like that may wake up some day in hell, where they're going to be jumped by a bunch of preachers who will scream, "You lied to us!" (That's your fault, honey, for being around the fire.)

And they, when they had heard that he was alive, and had been seen of her, believed not. After that he appeared in another form unto two of them, as they walked, and went into the country. And they went and told it unto the residue: neither believed they them. Afterward he appeared unto the eleven as they sat at meat, and upbraided them for their unbelief and hardness of heart. . . .

Some churches are so full of unbelief and hardness of heart that they don't even get excited when a leg grows out half an inch. It's because of hardness of heart. They're not being sensitive to people's needs. They're more worried about their appearance, bragging on their big church and their doctrine.

. . .Because they believed not them which had seen him after he was risen.

And he said unto them, Go ye into all the world, and preach the gospel to every creature. (Notice that Jesus didn't tell them to preach their pet doctrines.)

The Lord told me, "I'm restoring the gift of preaching." We don't have too many preachers left. We need some preachers who will preach the Gospel like T. L. Osborn and A. A. Allen did in their crusades. Brother Allen preached the Gospel. If you'd go to his meeting, you'd get healed.

They had resurrection power in those days. When they slapped you alongside the head, man, you got something! You don't get much in most churches today; maybe "a little dab will do you." They put a little dab of oil on the end of their finger and touch your forehead. Or they make the sign of the cross or some other religious symbol. When the Bible says to anoint people, it means to put some oil on them! If you're going to oil them, oil them good! And fresh oil is what the Church needs.

Church leaders will argue, "Now, we don't want the

Holy Ghost to get *too wild,* because we don't want to offend the banker who attends our church."

Offend him!

How many banks were around during the Depression? There were more churches than banks. Those stingy bankers had better understand that. They need a dose, not just a little dab, of some oil.

He that believeth and is baptized shall be saved; but he that believeth not shall be damned. That's pretty straight!

And these signs shall follow them that believe; In my name shall they cast out devils; they shall speak with new tongues. . . .

Signs! Too many people are running after signs. You aren't going to have any signs unless you're full of resurrection power. That's what Jesus was talking about. When you're full of resurrection power, you're going to have signs. *They are signs that you're full of resurrection power.*

And when you're full of resurrection power, people are going to be healed. They line up the sick in some churches, but nobody gets healed. They should be getting healed. Signs will follow you when you're full of resurrection power. If you've been with Jesus, you're going to have signs. The sign is: Do you have resurrection power, or not?

I know that's a different view. We always look at the miracles as a sign. But if you're full of resurrection power, miracles are going to happen everywhere you go. I'd rather have resurrection power than the sign. The sign will be there that I've been with Jesus and that I'm full of the Holy Ghost.

When you get over into the Acts of the Apostles (I like to call it the Acts of the Holy Ghost), you find that the whole city of Jerusalem knew that Peter and John had been with Jesus after the lame man was healed at the Beautiful Gate. Why? Because of the signs that followed them. They were full of resurrection power!

> **Now when they saw the boldness of Peter and John, and perceived that they were unlearned and ignorant men, they marvelled; and they took knowledge of them, that they had been with Jesus.**
>
> **And beholding the man which was healed standing with them, they could say nothing against it.**
>
> Acts 4:13,14

If you've been with Jesus, you've got resurrection power. But if your lustful eyes hang out of your head every time a woman walks into church, you haven't been with Jesus; you've been with the devil.

Now let's find out what finally happened to Peter in the second chapter of Acts. He had been a dead preacher. He had denied the Lord.

Today, preachers are denying the move of the Holy Ghost. They're denying intercession. They're removing all of E. W. Kenyon's books and Kenneth E. Hagin's books out of their library. And when they do, that's when the Holy Ghost is going to go out the back door, because they're taking the Bible out too.

They're saying, "We don't pray for the sick anymore, because we don't know if it's God's will to heal them or not."

My response to them is: The Holy Ghost isn't in you. You don't have any resurrection power in you. You're sitting around the fire, and you've become lazy. You've become a dead preacher, and your church has become dead — and you don't even know it.

The Lord came in my room one afternoon, and He told me the story of Peter. He preached it to me. He said, "The preachers are sitting around the fire, and people are walking by. They're saying, 'Aren't you word of faith? I remember you . . . Didn't you used to go to those Hagin Campmeetings?' 'Oh, no. Not me. I'm in another movement now.' "

Do you know what that movement is, honey? It's a *dead* movement. It's a *doctrine* movement.

We need to *repent*! We need to repent in order for the times of fresh oil — the resurrection power — to come.

A Move of the Holy Ghost

In Acts 2:1 we read, *And when the day of Pentecost was fully come, they were all with one accord in one place.* I like to say it this way: "And when the day of Pentecost was *finally* come," because God, Jesus, and the Holy Ghost were working to get that resurrection power back on the earth so men could be full of Jesus and full of Holy Ghost, resurrection power. And when the Day of Pentecost fully came, it was a *wave.*

And SUDDENLY there came a sound from heaven as of a rushing mighty wind, and it filled all the house where they were sitting (v. 2).

And SUDDENLY.... Our churches need a *sudden* move of the Holy Ghost! Preachers, of course, would have a nervous breakdown. But I pray the Holy Ghost will come in and take over their services, and those preachers will pass out.

And there appeared unto them cloven tongues like as of fire, and it sat upon each of them (v. 3).

Fire!

"Brother Ed, I really don't need to come to the prayer meeting anymore." You need some fire to burn out the sin in your life, honey.

"Well, I'm living with this gal, but it's all right. God will forgive us." You need some *fire* in your bedroom. I pray that every time you get together, fire comes into that room, your body starts shaking under the power of God, and you get so miserable you'll say, "My God, we've got to get married or something; I can't take it!"

In the Gospels, Peter was a wimpy, backslidden preacher sitting by the fire, denying the Lord (Luke 22:54-62). But in the

Book of Acts, we see that Peter was totally changed after the Day of Pentecost.

In Acts 3:1, we are told, *Now Peter and John went up together into the temple at the hour of prayer....* There's a miracle: two preachers together. The second miracle is two preachers going to prayer together.

But that's what happens when resurrection power comes into your life. You don't care what kind of preacher prays with you! You don't even care if the devil shows up! If he does, just tell him what you believe. Don't be like wimpy Peter and say, "I don't believe anything. I'm just sitting by this fire with this servant woman. I'm comfortable here. I'm not going over to where Jesus is, and I'm not going to admit that I'm hooked up with Him. Why, they're about ready to kill Him!" No, tell the devil what the Word says, and tell him what you believe. Say, "I don't believe what you say about my mother dying. I don't believe it!"

In the Book of Joel, the Lord promised to "pour out" His Spirit upon all flesh in the last days (Joel 2:28,29). Where is the Spirit of God? In us.

In these last days, God is going to pour resurrection power out of us onto the world. We're going to go out into the world clothed with His resurrection power. That's what happened to Peter and John in Acts 3: They got full of resurrection power and Jesus, through them, healed the lame man.

In Acts 3:2, we read, *And a certain man lame from his mother's womb was carried, whom they laid daily at the gate of the temple which is called Beautiful, to ask alms of them that entered into the temple.*

For more than 40 years this man had been a beggar at the Temple gate. His family laid him there daily. I believe the whole family was making a living off that one sick man.

A lot of people today are making money off of a sickness. Some people don't want to be healed because they would lose their pension money. I've asked them, "Are you collecting a pension?"

"Oh, yes."

"What happened?"

"Well, during the war I got hurt, and I got this injury."

"Do you want God to heal you?"

"Oh, yes."

"Well, are you going to write to the government and report that you've been healed?"

"Oh, no. I don't want to lose my pension!"

I have to tell them, "I can't pray for you, honey, because if you get healed and then you lie, you'll lose your healing — so there's no use in my praying for you." It's sad that people would want money instead of healing from God. When you get into people's pocketbooks, you find out where their heart really is.

When you preach truth, people don't like it. I know one preacher — John the Baptist — who got a man mad, and they cut his head off. King Herod didn't like John telling him he shouldn't have married his brother's wife (Mark 6:17-29).

If you preach the true Word of God, you aren't going to be able to sit by the fire where it's nice and comfortable. You'll have to go out where they'll want to cut your head off! But the good thing is that you won't go to hell, and you won't have a lot of people down there looking for you because you lied to them! I'm not going to be guilty of lying to people. I'm going to tell them the truth.

In Acts 3:3,4 we find that the lame man, ...*seeing Peter and John about to go into the temple asked an alms. And Peter, fastening his eyes upon him with John, said, Look on us.* People who are full of resurrection power say the same thing: "Look on us. We've got something!"

Christians today say, "Well, I'm a silent Christian. My

religion is *personal.*" Honey, if you've got resurrection power, you'll be out looking on people to get them healed and set free.

Back at the High Priest's house, before the Crucifixion, we saw Peter sitting with the women by the fire, denying the Lord. Now that he's got resurrection power, however, he's standing at the Gate Beautiful, saying, *"Look on us!"*

Why? Because God is faithful to His Word. He said He was going to pour out His Spirit on all flesh. And the only way it's going to get poured out is through you and me. God is pouring His power out of His Spirit, which is in you and me. Aren't you glad that you're a "spout" God is going to use to pour His resurrection power through?

There's a world out there waiting for you to say, "Look on us!" They're not waiting for you to be a silent Christian. Peter didn't say, "We're silent. We're going to the Temple because our beliefs are personal." No, Peter said, *"Look on us!"* He said, "I've got some resurrection power. Besides that, I found out that I have power in that Name. There's resurrection power in that Name — the Name of Jesus!" And he said to the lame man, "In the Name of Jesus, rise up and walk!"

Notice Peter didn't say, "I *hope* it works." Instead, he reached down and grabbed the man, because he knew it *would* work. And when the man got to his feet, he was completely healed. Isn't that what the Bible says? Where's wimpy Peter now? He's full of Holy Ghost power!

That's what the Lord told me the Church needs: a shot of resurrection power. You can have all your dingy doctrines and deep revelations, but they won't help anyone. Jesus said to go into all the world with this resurrection power and preach the Gospel.

The Good News, or Gospel, is that you don't have to be sick any more; you don't have to be poor anymore; you don't have to be depressed anymore; and you don't even have to have a bad heart anymore, because God's got some extra parts up in heaven. He knew when Adam fell that we'd need some extra parts because we're not perfect. We make mistakes. And we won't be perfect until we get to heaven. Only the blood of Jesus makes us perfect. That's what makes us the righteousness of God. That's what gives us right-standing with God.

People say, "Who do you think you are, preaching like that?" I'll tell you who I am: I'm an ambassador. My Big Brother is Jesus, and He's given me a job to do as an ambassador.

I'm not from this world. I'm not part of this world. I'm from another country. I'm a foreigner. I'm just passing through with resurrection power, and I'm going to take everyone I can to heaven with me.

I'm not trying to build my little kingdom. I'm building God's kingdom.

Chapter 3
Operations of the Holy Ghost

And when the day of Pentecost was fully come, they were all with one accord in one place.

Acts 2:1

We haven't seen anything yet of what God is going to do on this planet. The Body of Christ has limited God.

We saw in the last chapter that there was a set time God had established for the Day of Pentecost to fully come. This time was planned in heaven. God had a plan, and finally the day came. Something happened on that day. Let's look at what Peter preached in Acts 3:19, after the Day of Pentecost:

Repent ye therefore, and be converted, that your sins may be blotted out, when the times of refreshing shall come from the presence of the Lord.

Repent ye therefore . . . If it says to repent, we need to repent! Before a revival comes, the Church must repent of its sins.

. . . When the times of refreshing shall come from the presence of the Lord. As we saw in Chapter 1, another translation says, "And when the times of recovery of breath come from the presence of the Lord." To me, the key words from Acts 2:1 are "fully come," and the key word from Acts 3:19 is "times."

There are times in God's plans when He has "refreshings" come on planet Earth. Times of refreshing . . . fully come. To me, this indicates that there are times when God will move in a revival situation and give a refreshing or a second breath to the Church.

I haven't been able to get this teaching out of my spirit for months now. Every time I study the Word, it comes back. The Lord says, "Tell them what's about to happen! Tell them what's coming! Tell them to get ready for it!"

Would you agree that the Day of Pentecost was a re-freshing time? This planet is still rocking and reeling over that day. The devil is still having a nervous breakdown over that day. That's why he tries so hard to get tongues out of the Church. That's why he tries so hard to get the gifts of the Holy Spirit out of Full Gospel churches.

Today there are many cities that need the power of the Living God to be unloaded on them, but it's going to take a people who will repent in order to get the job done — and not the way we want it done, but the way God wants it done.

At the turn of the century, John Alexander Dowie shook a whole city— Chicago — with the gifts of healings. In 1900, Charles F. Parham's Bible school students in Topeka, Kansas, were hungering for God. To fulfill a classroom assignment, they all concluded independently that the biblical evidence of having received the baptism in the Holy Spirit had to be speaking in tongues.

At a watchnight service held on the last day of the year 1900, an 18-year-old, Agnes Ozman, got bold enough to ask Rev. Parham to lay his hands on her to receive the Holy Spirit. As midnight approached, and the twentieth century was about to begin, Rev. Parham finally agreed to her request. As he did, she was filled with the Spirit and began to speak in tongues. It was now January 1, 1901. A mini-revival soon broke out. And Miss Ozman wasn't able to speak English for three days!

Rev. Parham asked the Lord for "the same blessing" the night of January 3 in a service at the Free Methodist Church in Topeka, and he, too, was filled with the Spirit, speaking in tongues "until the morning."

In 1905, Brother Parham moved his Bible school to Houston, where one of his students was William J. "Daddy" Seymour, a black Holiness preacher. In 1906, Brother Seymour went to Los Angeles to preach at a Nazarene church. He was thrown out for preaching about the baptism in the Holy Spirit and speaking in tongues — even though he had not yet had the experience himself. He ended up holding services in an abandoned former church on Azusa Street. Daddy Seymour and other saints gathered in fervent prayer for revival. Refreshing came! The mighty Azusa Street Revival that broke out there in 1906 is still shaking this world today. All the major Full Gospel denominations were born out of that movement — because a black man was on his knees, hungry for God!

The Azusa Street Revival spread into many nations. Twenty years went by, and leaders like John G. Lake, Aimee Semple McPherson, and Smith Wigglesworth came on the scene to keep the revival going. (I recommend that you buy their books. They will inspire your faith.)

That move started to wane right after World War II. The breath was knocked out of us; we needed fresh oil. The Healing Revival broke out in 1947 and went across the land and around the world. Men like Jack Coe, Kenneth E. Hagin, T. L. Osborn, and Oral Roberts came out of that wave. The Voice of Healing, an organization of healing evangelists led by Gordon Lindsay, also was raised up.

Tremendous miracles happened when that fresh oil started to flow. Even ministers not specifically called into a healing ministry would pray for the sick and people would be healed. And out of that wave came the Charismatic Movement and the Word of Faith Movement in 1967, for 20 more years had gone by, and we needed another shot in the arm. The year 1987 was a marked year for this wave.

Don't misunderstand me: We're not doing away with the gifts of the Spirit that came out of the Healing Movement, or the teaching that came out of the Word of Faith and

Charismatic Movements. But if this is the last wave, I believe it's going to include all the waves from the Day of Pentecost up to the present in one giant wave.

The Lord told me that a recovery of breath of the gifts of the Spirit and healing is coming to the Church. *Healings always bring revival!*

Churches need this recovery of breath. They're going through the motions, but there's no power or glory.

The Sleeping Giant

Tommy Hicks, an evangelist during the Healing Revival, who is now a pastor in Buffalo, New York, had a vision years ago. He saw a giant lying on the earth. The giant was alive but dormant. Evil spirits that looked like spiders were holding this giant down. And every time a wave of anointing would hit the earth, the giant would shake himself.

Then Brother Hicks saw liquid fire come down from heaven and hit the giant — and the giant came alive! He shook those evil spirits off — and then the giant turned into millions of people. And the Lord said, "That's the Body of Christ." When the liquid fire or light hit the Body of Christ, the individual members dispersed. Phenomenal miracles happened, and a revival broke out across this planet that the world has never seen. I don't know about you, but I want to ride this wave in!

Churches have got to be careful. Now that we're respected and we've got nice churches on "the right side of the tracks," our pastors and leaders may start saying, "We don't want to shake anybody up. The Holy Ghost isn't for us to play with. We'll only allow the gifts to operate in believers' meetings." (I heard remarks like that in the Full Gospel church I attended years ago.)

The Holy Ghost *should* be moving in your community! He *should* be moving in your everyday life! He *should* be moving in your business!

32

I wake up in the middle of the night and sense that this wave is coming! *It's coming!* It burns in me! It gets into my preaching. It gets into my conversation. It's all I want to talk about. This wave is going to be something else!

I always stay with something until God releases me. Saying it *once* isn't enough. Saying it *twice* isn't enough. I've got to keep saying it until an awareness of the coming wave gets into the Body of Christ. That's my job! I go from church to church, and I've got to be in tune with what the Spirit of God is saying to the churches.

Discerning the Body of Christ

But let a man examine himself, and so let him eat of that bread, and drink of that cup.

For he that eateth and drinketh unworthily, eateth and drinketh damnation to himself, not discerning the Lord's body.

For this cause many are weak [wimps] **and sickly among you, and many sleep** [or many die].

1 Corinthians 11:28-30

I want you to realize that you can't divide the eleventh through the fourteenth chapters of First Corinthians. They must be studied together. Paul is talking here about discerning the Body of Christ and the gifts of the Spirit.

In the twelfth chapter, Paul tells us we are to discern our part in the Body of Christ. The reason why there are so many wimpy Christians is because they don't know where they belong in the Body of Christ. Instead, they float around from church to church, following fire balls, clouds, and everything else. They search for a word from the Lord when they really need to get in their Bible and get that Word in them first!

I've had them in my church in Los Angeles. They would say, "I'm tired of going to such-and-such church. They disciplined me. I was just trying to tell them I'm a fruit inspector for God!"

They don't discern their part in the Body of Christ. That's why they're weak, spiritually speaking — and many are dead spiritually. Until you find out where you belong and get to work, you'll always go from problem to problem and trial to trial.

Another failing among Christians today is that they do not discern the gifts of the Spirit in the Body of Christ. This is why so many Christians are weak at the game of life. You can't fight the devil physically with your flesh! You have to fight him with spiritual weapons. And these weapons — the gifts of the Holy Spirit — have been given to you by the Holy Spirit.

I believe that a revival of the gifts of the Spirit is going to be an important part of the coming revival. We're going to have more knowledge about the gifts of the Spirit than we've ever had before.

When I asked the Lord why we hadn't known more about the gifts in the past, He said that He couldn't reveal these things to us "because of carnality."

Until now, we've only scratched the surface on the subject of the gifts of the Spirit. We've had only limited teaching about these gifts, including the working of miracles.

Look at First Corinthians 12:1: *Now concerning spiritual gifts, brethren, I would not have you ignorant.* But that isn't the way I read it. I mark the word "gifts" out, because it was added by the translators. Now it says, "Now concerning spiritual, brethren, I would not have you stupid."

You see, Paul is talking about discerning the gifts of the Spirit in the Body of Christ. He doesn't want us to be ignorant concerning spiritual things, but the Body of Christ really is ignorant about them.

For example, sometimes when Brother Hagin is ministering and he gets ready to prophesy, everybody starts clapping — and the anointing leaves him! We're still carnal.

We've got so much more to learn about how to flow in the gifts of the Spirit!

I had to use the gifts of the Spirit recently in real estate transactions and dealing with the city when we built our Healing Production Center in Tulsa. In the past, I didn't always listen to the Holy Ghost, and I failed desperately in some areas because of my disobedience.

We're spiritual beings made in the image of God, and we should be creative — not just barely making it through life. Local churches should take an active part in their communities, taking those cities for God by using the gifts of the Spirit.

God's pastors don't need to be failures. If the people won't help him, instead of having to use gimmicks to raise money, the pastor can lie in bed and God can give him a word of wisdom, showing him, "This is how you can get the money you need." (If I weren't called to preach, that's how I'd be successful: I'd listen to the Holy Ghost.)

When the gifts of healings are in operation, a revival of healing will break out, like it did in the days of the Healing Revival. Mark and Janet Brazee and my wife, Nancy, and I were reading some 1948 issues of the *Healing Waters* magazine published by Oral Roberts. In those magazines we saw accounts of the tremendous miracles that took place.

Brother Roberts had a tent that seated 10,000 people, and he would have to turn 2,000 or 3,000 away sometimes. It reminded us of a statement Brother Hagin made concerning that Healing Revival. Brother Hagin said it was so easy to get people healed during that revival.

I believe that's what we're going to see in this next wave. And that's why God has instructed Mark and me to hold healing clinics across the land.

We've been kicked out of a few churches because they didn't want the Holy Ghost to move. They're set in *their* ways, and they don't want *His* ways. And **some** of those churches aren't going to go with this next wave because they won't go with the Holy Ghost's ways.

Personally, I've quit trying to figure out how every meeting is going to be. I just get before God and pray for the meeting, and then let the Holy Ghost move. In Holy Ghost meetings, you can say only one word by the anointing of the Holy Ghost and get people healed and set free.

Recently in Washington, D.C., I said, "Somebody get up and shout," and six black people got up and almost trampled me. I had to stand on the platform, because they were running all over the place — people were being healed by the power of God.

Administrations, Operations, Manifestations

Now let's look at First Corinthians 12:4-7

> **Now there are diversities of gifts, but the same Spirit.**
>
> **And there are differences of ADMINISTRATIONS, but the same LORD.**
>
> **And there are diversities of OPERATIONS, but it is the same GOD which worketh all in all.**
>
> **But the MANIFESTATION of the SPIRIT is given to every man to profit withal.**

Notice that the Lord Jesus is the One who *administers,* God is the One who *operates* the gifts of the Spirit, but the Holy Spirit is the One who *manifests* the gifts through the Body of Christ: *administrations, operations,* and *manifestations.*

How many remember that in Acts 2:17, Peter quotes Joel's prophecy: *And it shall come to pass in the last days, saith God, I will pour out of my Spirit upon all flesh: and your sons and your daughters shall prophesy, and your young men shall see visions, and your old men shall dream dreams.*

I believe God is going to pour out of the Body of Christ onto this world — *out of you and me.* Suddenly in a grocery store, God will start pouring out, and He will lead you to a certain person. This happened to me once. The Holy Ghost said, "That woman's ankle was severely injured in an accident four years ago, but I'm going to heal it right now. You tell her what's wrong with her ankle, and I will heal her. Let Me pray for her."

I told her this and she said, "Oh, no."

But the Holy Ghost grabbed her foot and started straightening it! So I said, "Let me introduce you to my Jesus, the One who healed you."

The poor devil's taking a double Valium pill right now! Do you know what I do sometimes just to torment him? I pull up a chair and say, "I bind you, devil, and I command you to sit in this chair." And then I preach to him for an hour and a half, and he has a nevous breakdown. I say, "You can't have this church. You can't have their finances." And he says, "Give me another Valium! Give me another Valium!"

That's what some of you ought to do. You ought to pull up a chair and say, "I bind you, devil, in the Name of Jesus. You sit down there. I want to tell you what I believe."

You need to tell the devil what you believe. You may need to say something like this: "I'm telling you, I'm healed, Mr. Devil! Did you hear that? That's the Bible. By His stripes I was healed. In the Name of Jesus, I'm healed by His stripes. I want you to know, *I'm not going to die! Grandma isn't going to die! And you can't have my children!* I believe on the Lord Jesus Christ, and my house shall be saved!"

The Word will give the devil a nervous breakdown. He doesn't care what church you go to; it's the Word of God that will defeat him. You'll hear him cry, "Oh, give me another Valium — I'm having a nervous breakdown!"

Administrations, operations, and *manifestations* . . .

Nancy has been studying the famous evangelist Maria Woodworth-Etter and her books. We'll be in a hotel room

and Nancy will say, "Look at this! Look at this!" She'll sit
there and jab me — and when she jabs, she jabs! I've had no
choice: I got interested in that book and Mrs. Etter's ministry. God was trying to get my attention.

God said to me, "This wave is going to be like it was in
her wave, when people 50 to 100 miles away will fall out
under the power and will see a vision of heaven and hell."

I said, "Now wait a minute — a sinner having a vision?"
(I'm not a "religious" person, but I thought only Christians
could have visions.)

The Lord replied, "What about Dr. Sumrall?"

I said, "But he was a kid dying of tuberculosis — and he
was a sinner — when he had that vision of the coffin on one
side of his bed and the open Bible on the other side, and You
made him choose between dying or preaching the Gospel."

And then the scripture came to me, "your young men
shall see visions . . ." God is going to give sinners a vision
of heaven and hell and tell them to make their choice.

We can't comprehend the mercy of the Living God!
We're not God's judges on this earth. God is going to use
the Body of Christ to reach the world. That's why He gave
Tommy Hicks that vision. That's why we must start learn-
ing more about the gifts of the Spirit. We've got to be more
sensitive to the Holy Ghost.

Do you know what it's going to take to have revival
come to our cities? We're going to have to pray like those
people who were hungry for God did in the early 1900s.
They said, "God, we repent of our own ways. We've gotten
into our ruts and said, 'This is the way we want it.' But,
God, what do *You* want?"

The Church needs a fresh breath. We need fresh oil from
heaven. We've had the greatest evangelists and teachers in
the world on television, but we haven't moved America yet.
I know not everyone is going to get saved, but we haven't
even scratched the surface!

Wait until you see a man of God who is full of the Holy Ghost on TV and he says, "Be healed!" — and the healing anointing goes out through the air waves and people in whole cities fall out under the power of God. When God breathes on you, look out!

Wait until you see church services turn out to be like old-fashioned tent meetings, with people being healed all over the building by the power of the Living God.

Wait until the preacher gets up and starts his "Six Steps to Success," and he can't even get to the first point, because the Holy Ghost starts moving in the service.

It's true. It's going to happen.

The Monk Who Went to Hell

We need to learn about *operations*. That just keeps coming up in my spirit. I keep reading about the operations of God, so I asked Him, "What's an operation?"

He reminded me of a Jesuit priest I met at a Full Gospel Business Men's meeting when I first started out in the ministry. At that time, I used to hold meetings in school auditoriums, preaching on healing and praying for the sick. We had some good results, and this former Jesuit priest, who was about 80, came to some of these meetings.

He walked up to me one day and said, "You sound like Smith Wigglesworth."

I replied, "How do you know that?"

He said, "Because I used to hold his coat."

I said, "Sit down." I pulled up a chair. "I want to talk to you."

I'm hungry for information like that. When someone says they knew some great man or woman of God, I want to find out what they know.

The man told me, "Smith Wigglesworth went all up and down the West Coast preaching, and I helped him. But,

Brother Ed, before I met him, I died and went to hell."

"How did you die?" I asked.

He parted his hair and showed me a big scar on top of his head. He told me he was praying in the monastery garden one day, and a storm came up. A bolt of lightning hit him right on top of his head, split his head open — and killed him.

I jumped back and said, "You mean *dead?*"

"Oh, yes. I was killed deader than a doornail."

I couldn't wait to hear what came next. I like stories like that. I like fast cars. I like fast airplanes. I like anything that has to do with fire and excitement. That's why I can't wait to ride in God's chariots!

The man continued, "That thing killed me, and I went down, down, down, down, until I came to a plateau. Two evil spirits grabbed me and put me into a long line of people. I saw this line of people, and I saw fire coming out of a pit. As the demons pushed people into the pit, the people would scream and yell. It was the most horrible thing I'd ever seen!

"As I walked along in that line, I said, 'God, I didn't know! I thought I was doing the right thing.' The two people in front of me fell into the pit. Then it was my turn. I was still saying, 'God, I didn't know,' when all of a sudden a bright light appeared and shone on me. I heard a Voice say, 'Stop!' The demons stood back, and I started going back up."

The man said he saw himself come back into his body. When he returned to life, he was speaking in tongues. He sat up and found that a sheet was wrapped around his body. He said, "They had embalmed me. I had been dead for four days." And he showed me the scars where they had embalmed him. (That's easy for God; do you think embalming fluid is going to stop Him?)

So he walked through the mortuary, still wrapped in his white sheet, and people screamed and ran. He walked back to the monastery and knocked on the big wooden door.

Another monk opened the door. This man kept saying, "I've been filled with the Holy Ghost. I've been filled with the Holy Ghost!" The monk stared at him and said, "You've got some kind of ghost" — and slammed the door in his face. (That's the kind of "ghost" I want: the resurrection power of the Holy Ghost in me.)

We don't know the mercy of God. We don't know a person's heart. You think because someone blew his brains out, he went to hell. Who are you to judge that? You can be sick in your head just like you can be sick in your body. You can love God in your heart, and your mind can be "out to lunch."

I know this is so, because I once preached for six months, and I still don't remember where I went, I was so hurt and wounded emotionally. I just got up and preached by the Holy Ghost. Praise God for the Holy Ghost! The Holy Ghost will show you that God doesn't always need that muscle called your brain.

After the former monk told me his story, I asked someone, "Is this guy for real?"

He said, "Oh, yes. He's been around for years. He's been kicked out of every Full Gospel church around here, and he's already outlived three wives. See that beautiful girl over there? He's married to her." (She was a Pentecostal girl about 23 with a bun on her head and everything.)

The man added, "That man is full of the Holy Ghost. He wins more people to the Lord than anyone I know. See that new Cadillac out there? God told him to go down to the Cadillac dealer and God would give him a new car. He shared his testimony, and the guy started laughing and crying. He said, 'Here are the keys for that car.' Things like that happen to him all the time."

The former monk told me that he was on a train one day in Oregon when God said, "Go back to the caboose and jump off when you go by the big pile of sawdust." So he ran to the back of the train and jumped off into the sawdust. The train went about a mile farther and everyone on board was killed in a head-on collision. But he was spared because he obeyed what the Holy Ghost said.

Listen to the Holy Ghost

There are a lot of Christians in graveyards today who wouldn't be dead if they had listened to the Holy Ghost. But the Holy Ghost will not only save our lives; He will also make us prosperous if we will listen to Him.

People will say, "Well, you know, Brother Ed, I don't want to get too funky here." You *need* to get funky, honey — funky with the Holy Ghost.

We've been so scared that we're going to get in the flesh or get a wrong spirit, that we haven't allowed the Holy Ghost to move!

I've been in churches where the power of God hit the pastor's wife and she would start dancing. Then she turned red, was embarrassed, and stopped dancing. But Holy Ghost dancing and laughter are good for you! Some of you haven't laughed in years. Laughter is good for your bones. It's healing for your body.

So what if the devil points out that your checkbook is empty — you don't have any groceries in the cupboard — and your car's out of gas. Go out on the front lawn and say, "Ha, ha, ha, devil!" Laugh at him. God can breathe out of His left nostril on you and make you a millionaire overnight.

What are you worried about? God is God. He's the God of the Day of Pentecost. He's the God of the 1907 wave. He's the God of the 1927 wave. He's the God of the 1947 wave. He's the God of the 1967 wave. And He's going to be the God of the next wave. He's Smith Wigglesworth's God.

He's Aimee Semple McPherson's God. He's Ed Dufresne's God. And He's *your* God.

I want God to be all over me — in my mouth, my ears, and my eyes. I just want to be filled with the Holy Ghost and power — with demonstration and power. I want to be like Smith Wigglesworth, who could walk into a railway car, sit down, and the passengers would be convicted and cry out to God just because he was present.

Nobody gets convicted in a lot of our churches. Your worldly friends don't even get convicted when you go to their parties. They don't get convicted when you say, "Come to my church." They say, "Oh, forget it. You've got the same problems I have."

But when you're full of Holy Ghost power, they'll get convicted. I've been in an airport, sat down, and the stranger next to me jumped up and ran off in a panic because he was full of the devil.

What happened to the former monk who went to hell? It was an *operation* of God. God said, "Stop," the demons had to back off, and the man returned to life.

What happened in Mrs. Etter's miraculous meetings? *(1) God would operate; (2) Jesus would administrate; and (3) the Holy Ghost would manifest* through her ministry. I believe the Holy Ghost is going to manifest through the Body of Christ in this way. How many of you are hungry for God to operate through you? Tell Him, "Operate through me, Father. Operate through me." But we've got to repent of our ways to do it. We can't do what the world does and have God operate through us.

I'm not comfortable in hotel rooms anymore where they have cable television boxes. I can feel those evil spirits and what people are doing in those rooms. I don't want to spend half my time running the devils out of my hotel room, cleansing it.

So I'm believing God for a bus. When I travel, I'll live in the bus and know that the Holy Ghost is in the tailpipe, the gas tank, the walls, the seats, and everywhere else He could be.

You should be that way about the church you attend. You need to go to a church where the Holy Ghost is all over the platform and the walls. (In most churches, it usually takes us three days to fight through the religious spirits before the Holy Ghost can flow. Then we have to fight through the devils we stirred up when Sister Bucketmouth got offended.)

When the Holy Ghost is manifested through the Body of Christ, the Church will go out and do miracles and exploits by the gifts of the Spirit. You businessmen will know who to do business with and who to avoid. God will tell you what to bid for jobs you want to contract. When your contractor wants a crook to get the job, and he's counting on receiving a kickback, you'll know what they are doing. It's not cheating when you know that; it's winning.

Operations of God are the workings of miracles: putting a limb where there was no limb; putting an ear drum where there was no ear drum. We need more operations of God in our cities. We need the power of God to move into our cities, and I believe it will.

When I attended the National Religious Broadcasters' convention this year in Washington, D.C., I viewed a videotape of one of Brother Reinhard Bonnke's crusades in Africa, where people fell under the power of God in waves. And God said, "That's what you're going to see in America" — operations of God. Pastors will flow in the Holy Ghost, and you won't be able to understand it in the natural.

Years ago, I had a vision I didn't understand, but I understand it now. The head of Jesus was going around the globe, and He was saying, "Where is My Body? Where is

My Body?" In the vision, I started seeing the neck come together, and then the shoulders, the arms, and the rest of the Body.

The Body of Christ is coming together, and we're going to function properly and go around planet Earth with the power of the Living God before Jesus returns!

Chapter 4
The Operations of God

An interesting thing happened to me years and years ago when God was training me for the healing ministry. I was attending a Full Gospel church. ("Full Gospel" means they're supposed to believe the whole Bible.) I had just helped them build a new building, I was serving as a deacon, and I had made the decision to stay in that church.

Then I got hold of a book called *Healing the Sick* by T. L. Osborn, and it got me in real trouble with my pastor.

He said, "Ed, I know T. L. Osborn. I've been in some of his services." Then he said, "Have you ever heard of Kenneth E. Hagin?"

I said, "Yes, vaguely. I've heard different people mention his name, and I think I've got one of his books."

The pastor continued, "Years ago, I lived in Texas, and each year we invited Brother Hagin to minister in our church. One day Brother Hagin and I were having lunch, and he noticed I had a big knot on my arm. (It was in the middle of summer and I was wearing a short-sleeved shirt.)

"Brother Hagin said to me, 'Brother, why don't you just curse that thing, and God will melt it away?' I told him, 'It's all right; the doctors say it isn't anything serious.' But he insisted, 'Why put up with it? Why don't you speak to it and it will die?' I kept saying no, and then Brother Hagin said, 'Well, how about if I just curse it?' and I agreed. And he cursed it and that thing disappeared."

Now, years later, this same pastor said to me, "I know Brother Hagin and T. L. Osborn, but, Ed, you don't want to get mixed up in that stuff!"

Mind you, this was a *Full Gospel* pastor whose denomination came out of the 1907 wave! He had just finished telling me how he got healed by Brother Hagin's teaching, and then he warned me not to get mixed up with it!

I'm going to get mixed up with people whose prayers make tumors disappear! If I had a tumor, I'd want to go where that mixed-up bunch was, how about you?

People say, "Don't mess with those Word people." Well, if they're having results, and their bills are being paid, and their bodies are being healed, I'd want to go over there and listen to what they've got to say.

Turn off that muscle that's in your skull. It's hard for me to understand why that pastor wouldn't accept Brother Hagin's teaching when he was healed under his ministry. Perhaps the only explanation is that he was influenced by a spirit of religion.

For five years I had worked hard in his church. Many people thought I was a hero. I took a year and a half off from my job to build them a beautiful, round church. I was the superintendent on the job, and I also was the worker on the job. At night I cleaned the toilets. I did everything without pay. I was Mr. Wonderful to the pastor and to the people of that church.

It's God's Will To Heal

But as soon as I got into the Word of God and found out that it was the will of God for me to be healed, I wasn't so popular anymore.

When I was a sinner, I was never sick. I hated sickness with a passion, because my mother was sick all the time, in and out of mental institutions. When I got into the Full Gospel church, I was sick all the time. They kept telling me, "God is trying to teach you something."

I had to take out extra insurance on my children. Blue Cross and I were in business together. I was paying so many premiums, I felt like I was part of the company. Then I learned that we didn't have to be sick. Who wants to serve a God who makes your mother sick? God isn't insane; it's the devil who's insane.

It almost broke my heart to be thrown out of that church. It took me two years to get over it. After I left, church members would phone me and say, "Would you come over and pray for me — but don't tell the pastor."

This was a *Full Gospel* church, not a Baptist church. They were supposed to believe in tongues and everything. But if anyone spoke out in tongues, they would usher them into the back room, saying, "This isn't a believers' meeting." (I'm in a believers' meeting all the time.)

One member in particular had criticized me up one side and down the other. But one time at midnight I heard a knock at the door. There stood the man who had criticized me.

"Brother Ed," he said, with tears in his eyes, "my dog got run over. I don't believe what you preach, but would you please pray for my dog?"

This man owned two Irish Setters. They were chasing one another, and one was run over by a truck. Its back was completely crushed. The man really loved this dog, so he took it first to the pastor, but the pastor said, "Well, just go put the dog to sleep." Then he brought the dog to me.

I'll never forget it as long as I live. I simply laid hands on that dog and said, "In the Name of Jesus..." and all of a sudden we heard bones cracking! They went back into place, and God healed that dog! *How much more are you worth than a dog?*

Operations of God

I've never before mentioned this incident, but it came to my mind as I was reading about the operations of God. I'm not against God healing dogs, cats, or anything else.

That man got turned onto the Word of God because God healed his dog! It was *an operation of God.* What does "operation" mean? It means to work to accomplish things.

We accomplished some things, because the testimony of the dog's healing spread, and before I knew it, my house was full of people! I started my own prayer meetings. And I couldn't even preach!

I'd use a tape recorder and play someone else's tapes on those big, 5-inch reels. For example, I'd let Kenneth Copeland preach on healing for an hour; then I'd pray for the sick. Miracles happened all over the place.

I always told the people in my prayer meetings, "I'm not called to preach. I'll never be able to get up in front of people and preach. I'll just pray for the sick." Then one day God told me to leave my tape recorder home!

My first sermon was an absolute mess. I was supposed to speak for a youth meeting in the Full Gospel church. When I walked to the front, I was shaking like a leaf, and all the young people laughed at me.

I chopped the message up so badly that I finally just turned around, walked out, slammed the door, went into another room, and threw my Bible down. I said, "God, don't You ever embarrass me like that again! I thought You said I was called." The power of God came into that room, and God said, *"I have anointed your lips; man hasn't."* He added, "Stay right here."

People started coming into that room. One boy said, "While you were speaking, my leg started moving, and it straightened out by the power of God!" Another said, "My hips started moving while I was sitting there." Many came in to report miracles.

God said, "See what I mean?"

What was it? It was *an operation of God* to accomplish something by the Spirit of God. Recently, the Lord said to me, "I am going to operate to accomplish things in cities."

There's so much more revelation knowledge we need to know about the operations of God! There are (1) *operations of the Spirit* of God that work through any believer, and then there are (2) *operations of ministries* that God will operate through a prophet, an apostle, or another fivefold ministry gift, to accomplish things — to get things done for people — to get people saved and delivered.

In Chapter 3, we saw where Paul talked about "differences of administrations" and "diversities of operations" in First Corinthians 12:5,6. (Another translation calls it "different ministries.")

In verse 28, Paul teaches, *And God hath set some in the church, first apostles, secondarily prophets, thirdly teachers, after that miracles, then gifts of healings, helps, governments, diversities of tongues.*

Notice that *teaching* is more important than *miracles.* Why? If you receive a miracle, but you go back to your dead church and don't get the right teaching, you'll lose your miracle. The devil will use the people in that dead church to talk you out of it!

Don't Criticize Ministries

Never, never criticize another person's ministry and how he operates or flows in it. I used to make fun of one television evangelist because I didn't like his voice. It sounded too feminine to me. I would sit in front of the TV set and judge him, even though I was watching miracles!

One day God asked me, "How many auditoriums have you filled?" He nailed me!

We're not to judge or compare one another. If you don't like the fellow, just turn him off — or beat the devil over the head by sending him an offering.

The way I operate is different from the way a pastor operates. Remember, there are different administrations, different operations, and different manifestations, as we saw in First Corinthians 12:5-7.

Even in the natural, our U.S. Presidents operated differently in their respective administrations because each had a different personality.

The same holds true in the spiritual realm. God operated differently through John Alexander Dowie's ministry, and Dowie moved the great city of Chicago for God. He built a little wooden tabernacle across from the entrance of the 1893 Chicago World's Fair, and he preached in it for a year. During Dowie's successful ministry in Chicago, he was arrested more than a hundred times in one year for "practicing medicine without a license"; however, he finally emerged victorious with public opinion on his side.

Dowie beat the courts every time he was arrested because he was his own lawyer, and he responded to the lawyers with answers that the Holy Ghost gave him. They finally quit arresting him after that year because he wore the courts out. The Holy Ghost knows what to say.

Through an operation of God, that man did miracles — notable miracles. What is a *notable* miracle? A miracle that makes people take notice. The only time people notice some churches is when they have a wreck and run into them! Our churches ought to be known by the miracles and the power of God — *the operations of God* — that take place in them. And it's coming in the next wave! We may as well get ready for it. When the power of God starts moving, you're going to be noted for the miracles that happen in your church.

Every time I go to Chicago, I get such a burden for that city! Dr. Sumrall now has a television station on the Wisconsin border, and it will reach Chicago. It's not far from Zion, Illinois, which is the town Dowie founded for his church members. Dowie actually foresaw a medium like television which could broadcast a minister's image and voice to distant cities. Think about that: Dowie had a vision of what Dr. Sumrall's doing right now over his television network!

God told me that it's going to take an operation of God to move the city of Chicago for God: one notable miracle. A notable miracle found in the Acts of the Apostles was when the lame man by the Gate Beautiful was healed by Peter and John — and the whole city of Jerusalem was stirred.

The ex-wimpy Peter, you will recall, once stood by a fire and denied the Lord to a young woman. (I don't know why men of God crumble to women sometimes, but they do.) She asked him, "Aren't you the man? Aren't you the man who was with Jesus?"

"Oh, no, not me. Not me."

"Aren't you the man who used to preach faith? I know you used to run around with Brother Hagin."

"Oh, no, not me."

That's the way many churches are right now. They're backing off from faith. They're backing off from the Word of God. They're backing off from healing. They're into having women dance around, supposedly to inspire worship.

I was in such a church recently, and they had their dancers come out and do their thing before I preached. I was reading a book that I was going to give away that night, and God said, "Look up and watch the congregation. What are they doing?" Everyone was watching those girls; they weren't giving God any praise.

What does that dancing breed? It breeds lust; that's what it breeds!

We must give God all the glory and all the praise; we must not take attention away from Him.

Message on the Rooftop

Now there are diversities of gifts, but the same Spirit.

And there are differences of administrations, but the same Lord.

And there are diversities of operations, but it is the same God which worketh all in all.

But the manifestation of the Spirit is given to every man to profit withal.

1 Corinthians 12:4-7

Years ago, when I was putting tile on the roof of that new church I was building, God spoke to me. An invitation to attend the World Convention of the Full Gospel Business Men's Fellowship International had come in the mail that day.

I didn't have any money. I'd been working as a volunteer on that church for a year and a half, and I didn't have a job. I was "eating behind Safeway," where they throw away day-old bread and good produce.

God said, "Sell your house. I want you at that meeting."

You know, it could be destined by God for you to be at a certain meeting at a certain time! The reason I'm mentioning that is because I feel in my heart that God is going to start operating through churches to get souls saved and bodies healed by the power of the living God, and it will be important that people be in a certain place at a certain time.

I knew it was the voice of God. I put my house up for sale, and it sold right away. Within 30 days the escrow closed, I moved into a rental house, and I got on an airplane and went to that 1971 Full Gospel Business Men's World Convention in Denver, Colorado. The year 1971 was when the Word of Faith wave really gained momentum.

Kenneth Copeland was one of the speakers at a session attended by about 1,000 young people. Oh, it was so wonderful and so rich! The other speakers were John Osteen and Kenneth E. Hagin.

I'll never forget it as long as I live: Brother Copeland preached to all the teenagers on the Covenant man, David.

54

He preached that you don't have to be sick anymore; you can use the Word of God and kill the giants in your life. He said that's what David did: He used his covenant and the Word of God and slew that giant.

I had never heard anything like it! In the Full Gospel church I went to, the pastor read from the *Reader's Digest*. (That's hurting for sermons, when you have to get them out of the *Reader's Digest!*)

Then Brother Copeland said, "Everyone who's called into the ministry, come down to the front."

I wasn't called to preach; I was just called to pray for the sick — I thought. I was sure he didn't mean me. But it was like someone picked me up out of my chair and threw me down the aisle! I still think it was an angel who pushed me up there. So there I stood with all those teenagers.

When God's in operation, something is about to happen. God is about to get something accomplished. We need the operations of God in our lives to get the things God has called us to do accomplished.

Brother Copeland came to me in that line, hit me on the side of the head, and I fell down. He stopped and said to me, "YOU'RE CALLED TO PREACH!"

I said, "I'm not supposed to be in this line in the first place."

When I came out of that service I was drunk in the Spirit. I took the elevator up to the lobby and saw Andre Crouch at his ministry's table. I knew him from a time we had both worked with Teen Challenge, so I asked him, "That preacher who spoke down there in the youth service — does he have any tapes?"

A blonde woman standing next to me reached into her purse and said, "Yes, he does. Here." It was Gloria Copeland. She handed me a pamphlet, and of course I ordered all her husband's tapes when I got home.

Brother Copeland was invited to speak at that convention at the last minute. He was just starting out, and he didn't even take any tapes with him. *But if he was invited to that convention to reach anyone, God intended that he reach me!* After I got home, I locked myself into a room and listened to his tapes. That's how I got turned onto the Word of God!

The Healing Power Comes

After Gloria handed me that pamphlet, I was so elated. I was just walking around the lobby, and out of the corner of my eye, I saw a woman lying on the floor, draped over two steps. She had been on her way into a women's meeting.

Archie Dennis, a Gospel singer, was standing beside her with his hands up, praising God. I hadn't seen anyone fall in my Full Gospel church, so I thought the woman had had a heart attack or something.

"What happened to her?" I asked.

Archie explained, "Well, she asked me to pray with her so she would be filled with the Holy Ghost, and I laid hands on her, and she got it, and she just fell out over those two steps."

By this time a crowd was milling around and pushing into us. If you ever want a crowd, just fall over on the floor and lie there awhile! There were about ten rows of people trying to see what had happened.

I said to myself, "Well, Lord, I hope You never do that to me!"

Bam! I fell out right next to that woman. Soon another woman was laid out alongside me, and then a huge woman who had been behind me fell right on top of me! Here I am, a Full Gospel deacon going to a church that came out of the 1907 wave, and I'm lying between two women with a big one on top of me!

As I lay there, God said to me, "I SAID YOU'RE CALLED TO PREACH, AND YOU WILL GO AROUND

THE WORLD WITH HEALING POWER!" Suddenly my hands started burning, and what felt like hot oil started coming out of them!

During the first part of my ministry, all I did was lay hands on people for healing, but that was a slightly different operation. I had never heard about *special anointings* in my church. (There was nothing about Acts 19:11,12 in the *Reader's Digest*.)

I lay there for awhile, and finally that big woman got up — thank God. There was such an odor to her! Then the others got up. When the power of God hits, sometimes rows of people will fall out, and that's what happened in that hotel lobby: Many people fell at the same time.

While I was lying there under the power, God was working on me to accomplish something. Some of you may think, "That can't be an operation of God." Don't criticize.

As I was brushing myself off, the big woman said, "Something happened to you." I said, "Yes, God said something about healing power being in my hands."

She said, "I knew it! Lay your hands on me, and I'll be healed!" Then she told me she had a big tumor — that's where the odor was coming from, and that's why she was so big and she was wearing a dress made like a tent.

When I laid my hands on her, I just said, "Be healed!"— and it sounded like the tumor popped and the dress shrank all at the same time. I went, "Oh!"

And all those people jumped back. I said, "My Lord!"

And a man 80 some years old came running up to me and said, "Young whippersnapper, you pray for me and I'll get the Holy Ghost! Then I can go home to be with Jesus. I've been seeking for 50 years now."

I said, "Speak"— and he started speaking in his heavenly language.

Then people came running to me from all over the lobby. I prayed for the sick, and tremendous miracles happened. And that's what got me kicked out of my church when I returned home.

For six months, outstanding miracles happened in my ministry: Scars disappeared, crossed eyes straightened. Then it started to wane, partly because I wasn't walking in love with the people in that church.

But Jesus said to me recently, "Miracles are going to start happening again in your ministry the way it was at the first." He explained that God couldn't trust me with that kind of power then, because I was still a baby Christian.

I'm not sharing that with you to brag. God put the anointing in my hands because God was operating, and He has a plan for my ministry. What is that plan? To accomplish things for the kingdom of God.

Grieving the Operations of God

God is going to start working through operations of the Spirit to take cities and even countries for God. Some ministers plant and some reap the harvest. The one who does the harvesting usually gets all the credit. We forget that God was in operation, working and accomplishing what was needed for that revival to start — and some little grandma who interceded for it for years will get a crown for it in heaven.

We give men too much glory. That's why the anointing will lift from a service when dancers in a praise service call attention to themselves.

We recently watched a prophet of God teaching about the glory of God on a Christian television program. The glory was there; you could actually see the smoke on your TV set.

Then an outstanding singer was asked to sing. He sang about Jesus, but we were all oohing and ahing over how great the singer was — and the glory left.

God said to me, "The glory left because we weren't giving Jesus all the praise."

The singer and audience didn't move in the glory. If we had, there could have been an operation of God that would have lasted for eternity! *We need to be taught to flow with the Holy Ghost when He is moving.*

We have so much to learn about First Corinthians 12 and about God's operations. We must learn how to be sensitive to God's Spirit! Get behind your pastor with your prayers so the operations of God will be in manifestation to accomplish things.

My experience in that hotel lobby happened sixteen years ago. Why? God was accomplishing something for my ministry. He had been building up to that experience.

Many of the Full Gospel people who made fun of me are dead today, but before they died, they called and asked me to pray for them.

And I didn't know it then, but God was accomplishing things in my life all those years: operations of God.

There's something here that God wants to get across to us: We must be more sensitive to the Spirit of God so we don't grieve the Spirit.

We must move into the realm of the Spirit in order for the glory of God to move into our churches and for the operations of God to win our cities for Him.

We must move into that other realm because more knowledge and more revelation are coming concerning the administrations, operations, and manifestations of God.

We must move into that other realm so we can flow one hundred percent in this revival. In the past there have been those who missed waves and revivals, but we must get into this one!

We must push into that realm of the Spirit! Many get right up to it, but it seems they just can't step across, and they are frustrated. But we must not be lazy; we must pray and seek God. Enoch got over into that realm. He walked with God, and they never found his body.

There's another realm of glory and another realm of the Spirit that men will walk in, in these days.

I will operate in the apostles, and the prophets, and the teachers, as I have set in the church apostles, prophets, and teachers — this is the order.

My apostles and my prophets will operate in a new realm, and they'll even bring revival to cities. It will even go to city hall; they will see the glory, and they will see the power.

There are men and women being raised up today — particularly men — who will operate in the office of a prophet.

Do not criticize because you do not understand; but there will be men I'll operate through as I did through men of old. They will do miracles, and they will do exploits and wonders.

I'll raise up prophets in cities who will prophesy and I will answer their prayers. I will hear their words; their words will not fall to the ground. And they won't bring glory to themselves, but to Me.

I am the God of fire. I am the God of glory. I am the God of miracles. I am the God of wonders. I am the God of cities.

There will be those who will flow in that other realm. Many will be criticized. Many will criticize them because they do not understand. They will not understand.

But there is another realm that I desire my men to walk in. Yes, I'll raise up exhorters. I'll raise up women to be exhorters and ministers who will operate under the healing anointing. But I will raise up the apostle and the prophet for this last revival.

As it was when the new came in, the apostles and the prophets laid the foundation with Jesus as the Chief Cornerstone. As it goes out, it will be the same: first apostles, then prophets will come on the scene.

Yes, this will be the wave of the apostle and the prophet. It has been the wave of the teacher — he has been on the forefront, and I needed those words to be spoken — but now to the forefront will come the apostle.

There will be many churches where the apostle will operate even as a pastor, and they'll go out, and they'll come back, and they'll go out, and they'll come back. And there will be those who will even come against my men who get into that realm of glory and walk under that power as Elijah and Elisha, and these men, and as even Enoch walked and talked with Me in that realm.

Very few men have walked in that realm, even in this generation, but you will see them be raised up. Yes, there is a new breed rising.

There are those who have been on the scene that I will take very shortly. They will be caught up, and they will come with Me. And they will be praised and they will be blessed for their work being well done.

But there are fresh anointings and another realm that men will walk in, and there will be those meetings where everyone will be healed by my power and my glory.

There are those who will walk in that other realm, but you must be very careful to walk holy and upright before Me.

The spirit of the world has gotten hold of my Church. There is no conviction in their hearts, because their hearts are seared. They'll say "Amen" to the glory, and they'll say "Amen" to the world; but they'll not be with those who will walk up in the mountain and in the glory with Me.

I'll show them things to come, and I'll show them the glory and how to walk in it. I'll teach them about the glory, and I'll teach them about the other realm.

Some of you will walk as an apostle and as a prophet, and you will speak, and it will come to pass.

I AM THAT I AM, and I pick, and I operate, and I administrate, and I manifest through whom I want. I put up, and I put down, and it's my desire to raise men to walk in that other realm.

There will be those who will be raised up as pastors, and there will be those who will walk in the gift ministries; but it will be particularly the apostle and the prophet through whom I will operate and do exploits.

Churches that will not allow or invite the prophet or the apostle to come will surely dry up, because they will not discern their part in the Body and in the Church, and they will become weak and worldly and dead.

But those who will discern the whole Body, and those who will discern the gifts of the Spirit, and those who will discern the gift ministries will be strong and well balanced.

And there will be a place for the pastors, which is in my Word. And there will be a place for the evangelists, which is in my Word. And there will be a place for the teacher, which is in my Word. And there will be a place for the prophet, which is in my Word. And there will be a place for the apostle, which is in my Word.

Things are changing, and heaven is getting ready for the homecoming.

There is one more home run to be hit, and it will be glorious, and then it will be time to come home to be with Me, saith the Lord. Prophecy delivered by Ed Dufresne

Paying the Price

Oh, the price you must pay to walk in that anointing and in that glory! Can't you see it — millions and millions and millions coming into the kingdom in this wave! Millions coming to know the Lord Jesus Christ!

The harvest is ripe, but God lacks the laborers who will pay the price. Oh, there are those who are hirelings, and they come for a paycheck, but they're not His true reapers. During this wave, His true reapers will come on the scene, and we will see the operations of God.

Chapter 5
The Double Portion

Do you know the story of Elisha and Elijah? Elisha was at the right place at the right time when Elijah's mantle fell.

The mantle doesn't *automatically* fall on a man of God just because his dad's a prophet. If the son is goofing off, doing his own thing, the mantle won't fall on him when his dad goes home to be with the Lord.

I believe you have to be in the right position with God, and you have to *want* that anointing more than anything in the world. Elisha wanted it that much, because he refused to leave Elijah. (He wouldn't even go to the local Bible school.)

When I was a young Christian, I couldn't figure this out. Then I started getting revelation knowledge about the relationship of Elijah and Elisha. I came to realize that you can receive a mantle through *association*.

I once worked alongside a pastor for five years, doing everything I could find to do — from janitor work to construction — in the ministry of helps. I didn't know then that I was called to be a pastor. I even told God that I wasn't a pastor. I considered myself to be strictly in the ministry of helps.

I always wondered where I got the anointing to be a pastor. The other day God said to me, "Because you helped that man build his church, and you were around him, the anointing to be a pastor came on you by association."

Some of you are running after a big anointing, and you're missing the whole thing. You should determine in your heart, "Bless God, I'm going to stick with this pastor and this church." You'll be surprised. One day God will look down and say, "I can trust him. I'll put the same anointing on him."

There's something wonderful about being around men of God, where the anointing is. I'm not lifting up the flesh by stating this; I'm simply recognizing the anointing of the Spirit of God on them.

Later, when I met men of God, the Lord told me to stay close to these men, so I started working with them. Then I got around Brother Hagin, and some of his anointing rubbed off on me.

Kenneth Hagin Jr. says that when I start flowing in the Holy Ghost, my ministry is similar to that of his father, Kenneth E. Hagin. Why? Because years ago in a meeting in Hawaii, Brother Hagin laid hands on me, and something was *imparted* to me; a stronger anointing came upon me. You see, a mantle can also be imparted by the *laying on of hands*.

Don't Get Sidetracked

And it came to pass, when the Lord would take up Elijah into heaven by a whirlwind, that Elijah went with Elisha from Gilgal.

And Elijah said unto Elisha, Tarry here, I pray thee; for the Lord hath sent me to Bethel. And Elisha said unto him, As the Lord liveth, and as thy soul liveth, I will not leave thee. So they went down to Bethel.

2 Kings 2:1,2

When you get an opportunity, study and meditate on this chapter of Second Kings. Every time you do, the Holy Spirit will reveal more truths to you.

Verse one tells us that Elijah went up into heaven "by a whirlwind"! Whirlwinds have come into a few of my services. I was taking a supernatural offering one time in

Bakersfield, and a whirlwind came out of the balcony and down through that church. It hit all the people who were giving in that offering, and God blessed them. Oh, we need more services where a whirlwind comes from heaven and blesses the people!

From verse two we learn that a person has to determine in his heart that he isn't going to leave the anointing of God, no matter how hard the devil tries to get him out of the ministry. And you can be sure that the *devil will do everything he can to sidetrack you from your ministry!*

He'll sneak up beside you, like he did to me once, and ask, "What are you doing cleaning this church building?"

I answered, "I'm obeying God! Bless God, I'm not going to leave this church until a stronger anointing gets on me!"

I also remember the time I drove all the way up to Oregon to preach. I had a beat-up Buick with bald tires, and those tires seemed to talk to me all night long, saying: "You fool, you fool, you fool..." Even worse, it was snowing outside, and the car heater wasn't working — no matter how much I kicked it!

The devil showed up again and said, "Why don't you quit? Why don't you quit? Why don't you quit?"

I said, "I want it too bad! I want that anointing too bad!"

I want to fellowship and walk with God so bad! I've tasted it, and I want to be part of God's plan. There are preachers who are far more capable than I am. There are silver-tongued teachers who can teach circles around me, but they don't have any meetings and I have more than I can fill, because they didn't want it bad enough. They didn't settle it in their hearts. They weren't determined.

You've got to determine in your heart when you go after something, you're going to stay with it and serve God, *no matter what.* If I hadn't determined this long ago, I would be knocked out of the race today.

Several years ago, I went through a situation where it seemed all of hell was released on me, but I remained faithful to God. Everything was taken away from me. I lost my home. God turned that situation around and gave me a better home. I lost my airplane. God gave me one that was paid for.

One day on my airplane, I looked around and said, "God, I didn't use my faith for this. Why did You give it to me?" And He said, "I'm testifying of the sacrificial giving in your life that showed you'll serve me no matter what. You haven't seen anything yet! They'll say across the land that the hand of God is on Ed Dufresne."

That's what God did for Abel, who brought a better sacrifice than Cain; God's still testifying today, 6,000 years later, of Abel's sacrificial giving. Abel gave his best. When you give your best, God will testify of your sacrificial giving too.

Waiting on a Ministry

Too many students graduate from Bible school only to end up in their old jobs again.

For example, an airport bus driver once said to me, "I know you! You're Brother Ed Dufresne. I heard you five years ago at Bible school, and you blessed my life."

I said, "How are you? And what are you doing now?"

He answered, "Well, I finished Bible school, but I'm 'on hold' right now, driving this bus."

Many men and women graduated with him from that same Bible school, and they're out in the ministry today. Why wasn't this man in the ministry? Something went wrong. He didn't determine in his heart to have an anointing on his life, and he fell prey to the devil.

The devil will throw anything he can in a minister's path — hardships or whatever — to try to sidetrack him and keep him from getting around the anointing. That's why many who are called into the ministry are still driving buses.

"Someday . . ." they say. But that day will never come. Now is the time to press in and give of your best! Now is the time to share the determination Elisha had for the ministry.

The Sons of the Prophets

> **And the sons of the prophets that were at Bethel came forth to Elisha, and said unto him, Knowest thou that the Lord will take away thy master from thy head to day? And he said, Yea, I know it; hold ye your peace.**
>
> **And Elijah said unto him, Elisha, tarry here, I pray thee, for the Lord hath sent me to Jericho. And he said, As the Lord liveth, and as thy soul liveth, I will not leave thee. So they came to Jericho.**
>
> **And the sons of the prophets that were at Jericho came to Elisha, and said unto him, Knowest thou that the Lord will take away thy master from thy head to day? And he answered, Yea, I know it; hold ye your peace.**
>
> **2 Kings 2:3-5**

Other prophets are mentioned in this story. It says they were "the sons of the prophets." I don't believe they were *physical* sons of prophets; I believe they were prophets called by the Spirit of God, and they were being trained by prophets in schools for prophets.

At the right time, some of these sons of the prophets were so superspiritual that they knew *by the Spirit* that Elijah was about to be taken up into heaven. But my brother and sister, you can know by the Spirit of God what is about to happen and still miss it!

They said to Elisha, "Don't you know your master's going home today?" And Elisha said, "Yes, I know it. Shut your mouth. I'm staying right beside him, and before he leaves, I'm going to get his mantle" (this is my translation).

> **And Elijah said unto him, Tarry, I pray thee, here;
> for the Lord hath sent me to Jordan. And he said, As
> the Lord liveth, and as thy soul liveth, I will not leave
> thee. And they two went on.**
>
> **2 Kings 2:6**

Elijah tested Elisha by deliberately trying to humiliate and discourage him. He would say, "Get away from me! Get out of here! Go on home!" But Elisha would answer, "No! As the Lord liveth, I'm going to serve you, and I'm going to stay with you" — and he wouldn't leave Elijah alone.

If we had some Elijahs today in our Bible schools — even Word Bible schools — the lazy students would get upset and leave. They have it too easy; someone else does all their praying for them. But in Elisha's life we see the kind of determination we should have. He insisted on staying by Elijah's side — "And they two went on."

Some of you have been floating around too long. You jump around from church to church, looking for someone to prophesy over you and push your button the right way. You've been prophesying hot air, and you won't hook up with a man of God and stick it out in his church until the anointing comes. Until you do, you won't amount to much, and you may end up shipwrecked. You ought to be getting into the Word and determining in your heart, "I will not leave the pastors of this church until the work God wants done is done in this city!"

> **And fifty men of the sons of the prophets went,
> and stood to view afar off: and they two stood by
> Jordan.**
>
> **2 Kings 2:7**

There were 50 men standing there, but only one stayed with the prophet of God and held his coat. Elisha probably had a family to take care of, too, but he was *determined* to get the prophet's anointing. I've heard the opinion of some Bible teachers that Elisha may have stayed with Elijah as long as 10 years.

Notice that even though the sons of the prophets were in school, they stood "afar off"! You can be in the middle of a move of God and still be "afar off." You can be "afar off" in a home meeting that is not watched over by a pastor. You can think you're a big prophet but be "afar off."

How bad do you want God to visit you? How bad do you want the anointing in your life, preachers? There are people even today who want the anointing, but they don't want it so bad they'll press in, whatever the cost. They'll say, "Oh, isn't that wonderful?" Then they'll back off, sit back, and criticize. That's what the 50 sons of the prophets did: They stood afar off and prophesied.

And that's what a certain preacher used to do to me. The devil would send him by the church I was helping build. He'd pull up to the construction site in his big, new car, playing tapes, and he'd watch us put in the foundation. Then he'd yell, "Brother Ed, what are you doing out there in that dirt? You ought to be a big-time preacher like me. Come on, man. Get out of that stuff. You've got an anointing on your life!"

But God had told me to get in that ditch and help build that church. I ran my maintenance business at night, and I went behind the Safeway store to collect day-old bread and vegetables to eat.

Like Elisha, I was determined in my heart that I was going to get an anointing on my life! I loved God too much to turn from the call.

And Elijah took his mantle, and wrapped it together, and smote the waters, and they were divided hither and thither, so that they two went over on dry ground.

And it came to pass, when they were gone over, that Elijah said unto Elisha, Ask what I shall do for thee, before I be taken away from thee. And Elisha said, I pray thee, let A DOUBLE PORTION of thy spirit be upon me.

And he said, Thou hast asked a hard thing: nevertheless, if thou see me when I am taken from thee, it shall be so unto thee; but if not, it shall not be so.

And it came to pass, as they still went on, and talked, that, behold, there appeared a chariot of fire, and horses of fire, and parted them both asunder; and Elijah went up by a whirlwind into heaven.

And Elisha saw it, and . . . he took up also the mantle of Elijah that fell from him . . . .

2 Kings 2:8-13

Anointing by Association

We see from these verses that your anointing can be stronger than the person's that you've been associated with. Elisha got *a double portion* of the anointing Elijah had!

Years ago, A. A. Allen had a tremendous healing ministry marked by great miracles. A man by the name of R. W. Schambach used to hold Allen's coat and be his "front man." Today Brother Schambach, who is also known for his tent meetings, has a stronger anointing than Brother Allen had.

Look at Jerry Savelle. He picked up his anointing from Kenneth Copeland. Brother Savelle used to carry Brother Copeland's coat. He also used to duplicate his tapes and get all the tape orders out at night while Ken slept. But there was a day when that double portion came on Jerry.

And it could happen to you! God is no respecter of persons. It doesn't matter how old or young you are. Look at Smith Wigglesworth: He was in his late 40's when his ministry got going — and he shook continents for God. We're still talking about his ministry.

Years ago, Brother Wigglesworth was a speaker in a meeting in England when he heard an American by the name of Lester Sumrall preach. Afterwards, Wigglesworth went up to him and said, "Listen, young man, you need to come over to my house. I need to talk to you." Their friendship began with that first meeting.

Brother Wigglesworth would read the Word of God to Brother Sumrall and pray with him. Then he'd say, "Now, young man, I'm going to bless you." And he'd stand up and bless him.

Do you know why Dr. Sumrall is so bold? He got Smith Wigglesworth's boldness! And do you know why so many preachers take Dr. Sumrall's trips to Israel? They want to be around him to get his anointing!

I've been around the world with Dr. Sumrall. I've sat next to him on airplanes and in airports. He's done the same thing for me that Smith Wigglesworth did for him. He's put his arms around me and read the Word to me. I like to be around him. I want the wisdom that man has.

Dr. Sumrall has said, "Brother Ed, the tragic thing is that when these great men of God get older, none of the young men go to visit them. I know there are a lot of young men who would like to have the anointing that is on my life, but not too many want to pay the price."

God spoke to Dr. Sumrall and said, "I want you to implant the anointing that's on your life into these young men." That's why God gave Dr. Sumrall a jet. He flies all over the country to preach in churches — but he goes to minister to the young pastors as well. He told me so.

Elijah told Elisha that he had asked for "a hard thing." It's a hard thing to be a prophet. (If it were easy, everyone could sit around and watch television all day, and a strong anointing would simply fall on their lives.)

Elijah added, "Nevertheless — because of your determination, and because you stayed with me even when I tried to shake you — if you see me when I am taken from you, it shall be so unto you; but if not, it shall not be so."

Elisha saw Elijah go up in the chariot of fire. Why didn't

those 50 sons of the prophets see it? Because they were afar off, *playing* at being prophets.

Today, prophets *are* moving out in the Spirit, and God is doing creative miracles in their ministries — yet pastors are criticizing them. They're standing afar off, like the sons of the prophets, and prophesying against the true prophets. They don't want to get into the move themselves because it isn't popular! A prophet's ministry is *never* popular.

This is where a lot of people miss it: They wouldn't recognize the anointing if it passed them in a red suit! We need ushers who recognize the anointing and flow with it. Too many ushers don't know the difference between the devil and the Holy Spirit moving on people. They need to know when to leave people alone when the power of God is working on them.

Young pastors miss a great deal if they think they know it all and refuse to invite older men to preach in their churches. Maybe you can't agree with them *completely* on doctrine, but there is still something you could learn from them.

> He took up also the mantle of Elijah that fell from him, and went back, and stood by the bank of Jordan.
>
> And he took the mantle of Elijah that fell from him, and smote the waters, and said, Where is the Lord God of Elijah? and when he also had smitten the waters, they parted hither and thither: and Elisha went over.
>
> And when the sons of the prophets which were to view at Jericho saw him, they said, The spirit of Elijah doth rest on Elisha. And they came to meet him, and bowed themselves to the ground before him.
>
> And they said unto him, Behold now, there be with thy servants fifty strong men; let them go, we pray thee, and seek thy master . . . .
>
> 2 Kings 2:13-16

The "Bless Me" Bunch

The sons of the prophets missed it, even though they were in Bible school. Why weren't they there beside Elijah, pressing in for his mantle, as Elisha was? They could have been there, but they didn't want to pay the price. They hadn't determined in their heart, "I'm going to have an anointing on my life when I come out of this school!"

They were too busy playing games, going to Charismatic meetings, and having Holy Ghost rubdowns, prophesying over one another in their "Bless Me Club"! They were saying, "You prophesy over me, and I'll prophesy over you. You prophesy that I'm great, and I'll prophesy over you that you're great!"

I had students like them in my training center in California. They wouldn't do anything to get the mantle. They wouldn't get involved. They wouldn't get around the man of God. They wouldn't offer to hold his coat. They wouldn't offer to help a pastor do anything. They wouldn't offer to clean the church toilets for Jesus.

They're the ones sitting on the back row today, waiting for the service to be over so they can pass out their business cards. They also sit at the employment office, moaning, "I don't understand it! I can't find any place to preach." Why? They weren't determined to get what they went after. (If you don't have anything to say, you aren't going to be invited to preach anyway.)

I also had students like Elisha in my training center. They worked hard in the ministry of helps, got around men of God to increase their anointing, and did whatever else they could to be involved. They determined in their hearts, "Bless God, I'm not leaving until I get that anointing!"

They would ask, "Ed, can we hold your coat? Can we drive you to a meeting?" They wanted to get around that anointing. They did pick up the anointing that is on me, and they are in the ministry today. They have big churches. In fact, some of them have a bigger church than I had!

But do you know what the "sons of the prophets" in my training center called the men who were like Elisha? "Kissies." They would sneer, "You kissies are just trying to get close to Ed." No, they were trying to get around that anointing!

After Elijah was taken up into heaven in the fiery chariot, the sons of the prophets camped out in the desert for three days, searching for his body. Of course, they never found it, because his body was not in a graveyard on this earth. Elijah was so wrapped up with God, he just took off!

There are a lot of people today who are looking for dead men's anointings! They say, "Oh, if I only had the anointing of William Branham!" There are people who are actually still chasing his anointing.

The man of God — Elisha — was there in their midst, but they went out chasing after a dead man's anointing!

Many people today are running around after dead men's anointings when there's a man of God in their own town! They ought to go and hold his coat. And if they have the ministry of making money, they ought to shovel it into his ministry.

The sons of the prophets came back worn out only to find that Elisha now had a double portion of Elijah's anointing — and he was splitting rivers and performing other miracles with that mantle!

That's what I'm after: splitting rivers! I want the power of God. And that's what the world is looking for too: Men and women who have the Holy Ghost and are full of His power.

When tragedy knocked on my door, and it looked like Ed Dufresne went down the tubes, the ones I thought were my friends ran off and prophesied, "Ed is finished."

God said, "Don't you move. You stay there." I stayed. The hurt was so bad, but I obeyed God. Then, when a stronger anointing came on me — *a double portion* that hadn't been there before — those same people said, "Ed, your ministry has changed. We were behind you all the time." Well, I just love them anyway.

Elisha was determined: He was hungry for that anointing. He had killed all his cattle and left everything to go and serve God. The other prophets missed it, but Elisha didn't. Elisha wanted that mantle, and he was determined to pay the price for that anointing.

Surviving the Rough Times

Are you that hungry for the anointing of God? Do you want to know why there aren't many Kathryn Kuhlmans in our pulpits?

There aren't enough people willing to *pay the price.*

There aren't enough people who can stand to be *persecuted.*

Young preachers today amaze me. They moan, "Oh, we just don't understand it! We did a few miracles and people *talked* about us." I always ask them, "Are you better than Jesus?" They talked about Him too.

Christians with an attitude like that give up when things get rough. I want to tell you something: The more you press in to the anointing — the more you walk in the Spirit — the stronger the anointing will become on your life, and the more pressure you will have to endure.

If you're going to operate in the power of God, you're going to be persecuted just like Jesus was. But you can follow Jesus' example, too, and walk right through your problems in the power of the Holy Ghost.

The people of Jesus' hometown, Nazareth, got mad and decided to throw Him off a cliff the day He got up and announced that His prophet's ministry had begun. But

Luke 4:30 says He passed, or walked, through the midst of them.

Another translation says, "He disappeared and showed up in the next city." I like that one! How would you like to be flowing in the Holy Ghost so much that you dissolve right in front of your enemies and show up in another city?

God said to me that some of the Word churches are trying to push the prophets off the cliff today: The prophets are speaking, but when they do, the people get mad and want to destroy them. God told me there are different ways to push prophets off a "cliff": stop their finances, start gossiping about them, and stop praying for them.

I'm hungry for the Holy Ghost! *People today aren't hungry enough for God!* They come to church only on Sunday morning, and that's it. They won't come during the week, and then they wonder why they're exhausted by Thursday. Then, when asked if they are coming to midweek services, they give the excuse, "I've got things to do."

Those sons of the prophets in Elisha's day were too busy also. They, too, were involved in church work. One was probably sweeping. One was cleaning the prophets' school. But they were all making fun of Elisha because he shined Elijah's sandals and stayed close to the prophet, content just to hold his mantle.

"You ought to come over here to our school and see how great it is," the sons of the prophets called out to Elisha. He replied, "Leave me alone." He wouldn't listen to his friends. He stayed with the prophet of God, and when the changing of the guard came — when a new move of God came — the mantle fell on him and he got it!

Look for the Changing of the Guard

Something new is happening. God has been telling me that some of His "generals" will soon be going home to be with the Lord, and there will be a changing of the guard.

He told me, "Move to Tulsa and get in position." People can read all kinds of things into that, but I am getting into position, and I am building what God told me to build.

What did God tell *you* to do? Don't be like those who say, "Oh, God did great things for us in the Word of Faith Movement. Bless God, we got a building, and this happened and that happened."

Don't build your little camp up on the beach! Get before God, and find your position. He may want you to get ready for the harvest by going down the street and building an auditorium that seats 10,000 people.

You're going to have to make a decision about what you're going to do with your life. Until now, you've been allowed to play church, but you're not going to be allowed to play church any longer.

You're going to see men and women flowing in the Holy Ghost to the extent that you aren't going to be able to even lie to them. You aren't going to be able to hoodwink them. You aren't going to be able to play your little religious tricks on them. You aren't going to be able to fool them with your church services that are in the flesh. They'll know by the Spirit of God that it's flesh!

Either you begin to work like Elisha, or you will miss out, like the sons of the prophets did.

"Work" is a word some people don't want to hear. Some Bible school graduates want to start at the top. They want to step right out of Bible school into an auditorium filled with 50,000 people!

After the school year had ended for our Bible school, I told one of the instructors, "Now, brother, during the summer we don't have any students, so we're going to put you in the ministry of helps."

He jumped out of his chair, stuttering, "I-I-I'm not going to be demoted! I am *a prophet!*"

I said, "I'm sorry. We have no openings for a prophet this summer. We've got too many prophets around here."

There's more to it than having head knowledge. I'm not against having head knowledge, but if you're not willing to pay the price for the anointing, you'll just be a dead, dry, head-knowledge preacher.

You must determine in your heart that *it doesn't matter what happens — you are going to preach!*

Kathryn Kuhlman and Kenneth E. Hagin are examples of people who were determined to have the "hard thing" — the anointing — regardless of the cost. Year after year, they held meetings all over the country, despite ridicule and rejection.

Brother Hagin kept preaching faith for years, with everyone telling him to shut up. He would rather have been home with his family, and he hated hotel rooms so much he wanted to kick the walls down — but he wanted the anointing, so he paid the price.

Do you love God? Are you determined to pay the price in order to go after "the hard thing"? You'll find that nothing's easy in the ministry, and you won't start at the top, but prove yourself faithful and God will promote you.

Chapter 6
The Prophets Are Coming!

I prophesy to you that *the prophets are coming!* Men and women of God are coming on the scene! God is assembling His army.

The prophets are coming to the land — prophets like Elijah and Elisha, who called fire down from heaven! You'll see sermons demonstrated when they get up to preach! God will move!

Limbs will appear where there were no limbs. Teeth will appear where there were no teeth. New hearts will appear where there were bad hearts. The prophets will speak healing to bodies. They'll even call fire down to burn up witches!

People will come to our services from all over when the fire of God and demonstrations of God's Spirit start to appear in our midst. *We need more fire!*

I've seen fire come on people in a few of my services. When it does, they get new hearts, livers, or other organs; and sometimes God gives them new teeth, or fills their existing teeth!

When I start preaching about this anointing — this fire — it comes on me. The glory gets all over me! The more I preach about it and the more I press in to it, the stronger it becomes.

Answering the Call

Every true prophet of God I've been around has a heavy anointing. The strongest anointing comes on me when I flow in what I'm supposed to do. For several years I tried it the other way, doing what I wanted to do when I wanted to do it. I found that it doesn't matter *what* we want to do. When we've got an anointing on our life, what matters is doing what God tells us to do.

Once I wasn't sure I was even called to the ministry, but now I know I am. If you're not sure, you'd better find out; otherwise, the devil will steal your call from you.

Some people describe the call as feeling like a blanket has been placed around them. Others will be praying for the sick when that blanket will come on them, and they'll know that a *stronger* anointing has come upon them.

After God calls you, and the anointing comes on you, you'll never be satisfied with whatever else you're doing until you surrender fully to that calling and flow in that anointing. Start by working in the ministry of helps in your church. Get involved and prove you're faithful.

There was a time early in my Christian walk when I didn't have any money, but I stayed in the ministry of helps because I was *determined* to do what God had told me to do.

I served as the church janitor and cleaned toilets for 4½ years: I had a toilet ministry! You talk about someone who needed to be humble and learn some things!

I can remember at least five times when I got so mad at God that I almost quit the toilet ministry. I had a maintenance business, cleaning offices late at night. During the day I cleaned the church and helped build a new sanctuary.

Getting Even With God

One night as I was cleaning an office building, I said to God, "I wonder how long I'm going to have to do this?" I was feeling rebellious and decided to get even with God. On the wall was a calender of a naked girl.

I said to myself, "I'm going to *stare* at that naked girl!" (I know some of you won't like that, but I'm just being honest, and this happened when I was a baby Christian.)

I thought I was getting even with God, but before I knew it, the power of conviction came on me and I dropped to my knees and repented. I tore that old calender up and threw it in the trash.

Then I made up my mind and said, "I don't care if it *is* for the rest of my life."

And God said, "I don't care if you do this the rest of your life either, because when you get to heaven, I'm going to lay my hands on you and say, 'Well done, good and faithful servant.' You'll get just as much reward as the pastor, or Billy Graham, or whoever you're helping."

I've tried to back off from the prophetic calling many times, but I get in trouble with God every time. Once I almost died. I ended up in a hospital bed with symptoms of heart trouble.

The doctors inserted dye into my veins, but they couldn't find anything wrong with my heart. Then they said, "We can't understand it. When we put you on the treadmill, your heart was almost ready to fail. It was in bad shape."

I asked, "God, what's wrong?"

He said, "You're finally in a place where I can talk to you! You've been rushing around, doing this and that. And when I tell you to speak, you won't, because of fear of men."

He added, "My angel came down and got on that treadmill with you and messed up the reading. The doctors told you there is nothing wrong with your heart. I knew it all the time; there *is* nothing wrong with your heart. But I had to get you into a position where I could talk to you."

Often we blame situations like this on the devil, but sometimes they happen because of our disobedience. A prophet can't allow a "hole" of disobedience like this to get into his ministry, because the devil will enter through it.

There are some things that the Lord has shown me by revelation that I'm going to have to say, or I'm a dead man. You will say, "Well, is God going to kill you, then?" No, my disobedience will kill me.

Spiritual Radar

I studied scriptures concerning the prophet's ministry a few days before attending one of Brother Hagin's seminars. You can't hide from Brother Hagin; he'll pick you up on his "spiritual radar." He detected me and said, "Ed, do you have something from the Spirit?"

I said, *"The prophets are coming! The prophets are coming."* These words kept coming from my spirit: "The prophets are coming! The prophets are coming!"

That's about all I said. A little later in that same service, Brother Hagin said, "I don't know what it is, but Ed's got something. Come up here."

Brother Copeland was sitting on the front row. He started speaking in tongues over me, and then he grabbed the mike. I knew exactly what God was telling me. Brother Copeland said, "Now, you're going to have to obey Me. You've almost died three times because of disobedience. You're going to have to obey Me and speak into that mike. Don't be fearful of men."

I got up in front of those people and said, "Yes, that's right," and then I told a little about how God had called me into the ministry in 1971 and had anointed me with the healing anointing.

I'm nothing special. I come from a family of alcoholics and people who were in and out of mental institutions. I was ready for one, too, before I met the Lord. But there's a determination in my heart to serve God. One reason is because *I love God.*

The Years in Hell

That determination and love kept me in the ministry during the years when it seemed like I was living in hell. I'd go out on the road, and I'd fight devils on the "front lines." When I came home, I had to fight the devil in my home. Then I had to fight the devil in the church I was pastoring.

I didn't understand it. Then God explained it to me. He started giving me revelation about walking in the Spirit — walking like Jesus walked. If you're going to walk like Jesus, you've got to have an anointing on your life like He had. But there's a price to pay for this anointing: The more you flow in the anointing, the more persecution will come; the more talk will come; the more the people will try to "push you off the cliff" to get rid of you like they tried to get rid of Jesus.

And if the strong men of God don't protect themselves — if there is any hole the devil can get in — he will try to destroy them and their families. That's why a lot of people say, "I don't want to pay that price." I'm not saying that your children have to die. The Lord has been giving me more revelation along these lines. Many of you know you've made mistakes and let the devil in. God was speaking to you all the time, warning you, but you weren't listening. The more you walk in the Spirit — the more you're in tune with God — the more you'll know what God is up to.

After sharing some of these things, I began to prophesy again. That's the way it works with me: After I start talking about it, prophecy just starts to flow out of my spirit.

Then I started talking about the prophet's ministry, and about how God wants to demonstrate sermons. God once said to me, "Churches, even Word churches, won't let Me demonstrate."

That's why there aren't too many real prophets around today. It isn't easy being a prophet. There's a price to pay. People get mad at you when God reveals that they're living in adultery, and everyone who is controlled by the devil wants to get rid of you! (Sometimes the devil even uses Christians to try to destroy the prophets.)

About two years ago I wouldn't admit I was a prophet; I wouldn't say a thing about my calling. I even said, "Now, Lord, I would rather be a *teacher*. Teachers are more popular than prophets." I thought I was trying to be humble, but I was also backing away from the prophet's anointing. God said, "You don't even believe in your own calling!" That cured me. I'm not ashamed of my calling now.

When I visit churches where they know and respect the prophet's office, they allow the prophetic anointing to flow, and there's a stronger anointing on me. In other places, they won't pull it out of me, and I have to limit my anointing to teaching.

The Church needs to hear what the Spirit is saying through the prophets!

A Big Dose of God

God once asked me, "Do you want to know why the Church needs the prophets, son?"

I said, "Why?"

He said, *"Because prophets bring a big dose of God."*

I'm not bragging on myself, but I get many letters from pastors after I've held a meeting in their church, and they say, "It seems like you *deposited* something in our church." I'll tell you what it is, and it's another reason why the Church needs the prophets:

Prophets tell God's secrets! They say what God's saying.

If we need to pray for anything, we need to pray for the prophets to come on the scene! But many churches — and I'm even talking about Word churches — don't want a prophet to come; or if they do allow him to preach and he says anything strong, they get upset. I've been thrown out of churches for obeying God. And some people won't support my ministry.

Why? Because when a prophet gets up and says hard things, it stirs up the carnality in Christians. They accuse him of being weird.

They say, "Bless God, we don't believe that! We don't want men of God to reveal what's going to happen, to tell about people going to heaven and coming back, or to tell God's secrets. We don't want to hear about people leaving their body. We don't want to hear about angels coming.

"We don't want to hear about things like that. We want you to tickle our ears and tell us we're going to get a Cadillac in the morning! We want to stand afar off and prophesy."

I got up in a meeting in Israel and said some things by the Spirit of God that must have read some people's "mail," because some of the preachers who were present later cancelled the meetings I was supposed to hold in their churches. They thought to themselves, "I don't want that guy coming to my church. He'll find out that I'm sleeping with the gal next door or something!"

We need to study to show ourselves approved unto God. Teachers, in particular, study. But when a church will allow a prophet to come and speak, he'll speak forth *revelation knowledge* that comes from the heart of God — knowledge he didn't get from any book, although it will be in line with the Word.

Many times in my meetings I have said things by the Spirit of God that I never studied. In the past year and a half, these revelations have been coming to me stronger than ever.

Stopping the Prophet's Message

The prophets are coming! God is grooming and setting aside men and women of God, getting them ready to proclaim His words.

But prophets' messages are not always well received. Even recently, prophets have been getting alone with God and then attempting to tell what God said — but people have been trying to shut them up and control them by withholding their financial support.

You'd be surprised how many churches caused two prophets I know to nearly quit the ministry. The churches stopped giving into these men's ministries and stopped inviting them to speak. Fortunately these men did not quit, but I was so grieved over their treatment that I asked God about it.

I said, "God what are You going to do about this? If I say some of the things You tell me to say, I know these churches will try to choke off my finances too!"

God replied, "If I have to, I'll make my prophets self-sufficient. If I have to, I'll give them all their own oil well!"

He continued, "There are thousands upon thousands upon thousands of pastors who are controlled by the spirit of the people, not by the Spirit of God."

Pray that our pastors will be controlled by God, not by people. God also told me that if people won't get behind their pastors, He'll get resources to them even if He has to send birds to feed them, as He did for Elijah.

Flow with your pastor. If you don't like what he's doing, you're signing up with the devil. Go down the street and cause trouble somewhere else. We don't need trouble-makers in the churches, and troublemakers won't last long in the next wave that's coming. Either they'll get out of the church, or the mortuary will get them — and I'm not saying that to be harsh or funny.

A prophet's ministry sometimes seems harsh because of the things he says. That's why a prophet is usually more popular after he's dead! It doesn't matter if you like the prophet's message or not; you ought to listen to what the prophet says. (You can always eat the hay and spit the sticks out. Some of you need to be poked with the sticks anyway.) Of course, I'm talking about a true prophet who will say what God is saying.

I'm not trying to be like anyone else. The more I get into the groove where God wants me to flow, the stronger my anointing is. I have to obey God; *I have to say what God tells me in secret.* When He says, "Tell it to the people," I have to tell it to the people.

If you're a carnal Christian, you won't like the things I say. There's too much carnality in churches today; even in Word churches. I'm sorry to say that some of the Word people are the biggest babies around. They think they're big shots when they're little shots — nothing but hot air.

They say, "Bless God, I've got my confession packet right here in my back pocket." But they're running grandmas off the road with their driving, and they're cussing their wife and hitting her over the head. They think they've arrived. They haven't arrived anywhere. They'll be lucky if God calls them to a toilet ministry!

He Gave Prophets

And God hath set some in the church, first apostles, secondarily prophets, thirdly teachers, after that miracles, then gifts of healings, helps, governments, diversities of tongues.

I Cor. 12:28

Notice what Paul says here. First, God gave *apostles*; second, *prophets*; third, *teachers*; and then *evangelists* and *pastors*. This is the order in which God gave the fivefold ministries to the Church.

Forty years ago in Pentecostal churches, they only recognized the *pastor* and the *evangelist*, and then William Branham came on the scene, and he was recognized as a *prophet*. When the Charismatic and Faith/Word Movements appeared in the last 20 years, the office of *teacher* was finally recognized.

Now we've had so much teaching, so much Greek, so many Bible translations, and so much faith preached to us that if everyone would release his faith at the same time, we could blow the United States off the globe!

We've been taught about the gifts of the Spirit. We've been taught about faith. We've been taught about moving in the Spirit. We have so highly esteemed the teaching ministry that we don't think we *need* prophets or apostles anymore; we only want to hear teachers.

Don't misunderstand me: I don't mean we don't need teachers. We *do* need teachers — and there are fine teachers on this earth today — but we've become prideful with all the teaching we've had.

Pray for the prophets to come!

Many Word churches don't want the other gift ministries to come to their church. They won't let a prophet come in and prophesy! Or if a prophet does come and flow in the Holy Ghost, they get upset! The pastor may say, "Bless God, we are a *Word* church, and all we're going to do is teach the *Word*." (The real reason he's upset is because he's jealous about all the attention the prophet is getting!)

Pastors must not become hardhearted or stiff-necked concerning the prophet's ministry. They must not forget that the prophet is the one who comes and speaks what God is saying. The prophet gives the church a dose of God — and that church is never the same!

I can say that because I've been on both sides: I've been a pastor, and I've been in the field ministry. Those in the field ministry shouldn't take advantage of the churches by bringing 25 people with them and running up big bills. So don't tell me I don't understand the pastor's ministry; I do.

However, I also understand the field ministry, and I've really been disturbed about the attitude in the Word churches concerning the prophet's ministry. When a prophet starts to flow in the Holy Ghost, a lot of people grumble, "We ain't going to have that in *our* church!"

That's exactly what most of the Pentecostal people said 20 years ago — and that's the reason their churches are so dead today.

Did you know that the prophet's ministry is really more important than the teacher's or pastor's ministry? Why is this so? It's so good the way the Lord defined it to me: *Because the prophet's a big dose of God! He comes and speaks what God is saying to the Church today.*

Let the prophets come!

Not for Sale

Big churches know how to get the big-name speakers: Offer them $10,000 and they'll come in a hurry. (But those speakers won't live very long.) Most of the men who go around saying, "I'm a prophet" can be bought for a price.

Of course, a true prophet (not one of those self-proclaimed prophets) is very careful to go only where God tells him to go. You can't buy him. He won't come to your church just for money.

You can't buy Ed Dufresne. You can't buy my anointing either. I've already been through that. I told you, I almost died for not acknowledging my anointing and walking in it.

If one pastor says, "Come to my church for $10,000" and another says, "I don't have many people, but will you come," and a prophet goes to the large church for the money — even though God told him to go to the small one — he is nothing but a prostitute, because he is a prophet with a price tag on him!

It's amazing. Some of these "prophets" have agents. I call them pimps. I don't need an agent. If no doors open for me to preach, I just go somewhere and pray and fast.

We need to get rid of our veneers, get down to the real

grain, be ourselves, and let God use us. I know that without God, I'm nothing. I don't have a good education. I really don't have what's considered to be the right personality to be a preacher.

Furthermore, I have no natural abilities to enable me to speak in public. So I have to depend totally on God! We may as well all go home if I don't have the anointing, for without it, I just hem and haw around. Yet God called me, and I am a prophet of God. I realize that the anointing in me is nothing to play with.

There's a great deal of teaching on faith today, but none on building character. We need to build character into Christians. Some Christians, including preachers, lie, cheat, and lack integrity.

God dealt with me about that too. He said, "Son, if you want to live to be 80-some years old (and if you ask Me for more years, I'll give you more), you're going to have to have some integrity about you. For example, you've got to keep your word."

The prophets are coming! Many of you, however, are looking only for deep revelations. And some of you are looking so deep, you're missing the whole vein.

Be careful: The spirit of the world wants you. The spirit of the antichrist has infiltrated the modern Church with humanistic teaching. I am appalled at how much humanistic teaching has gotten into Full Gospel churches— churches whose members ought to be listening to the Spirit of God.

I know, because I pastored for 8½ years. Married women would come to me and say, "Well, we want to abort the baby."

I would say, "That isn't what the Word says!"

"I don't care what the Word says," these women would reply. "I'm going to do what I want to do." Then they'd get mad at me and leave the church because I wouldn't back their decision. They were influenced by humanistic thinking.

There should be no question in your mind about abortion. You know better. I'm using the abortion issue as an example of how the spirit of the world has gotten on church members.

Those who have the spirit of the world will get mad at the pastor or prophet who gets up and preaches what the Word says about sin. They'll go down the street and find a minister who can be bought with a price; a minister who will take their tithe, pat them on the back, and tell them, "The way you're living is all right."

Pastors around the world: Stand up for what's right! Have some backbone! Don't let the people control you by threatening, "If you don't do what we want, we'll cut the finances off!" When you stand for what is right, God will take care of you, even if everyone leaves your church.

It's true that the bolder you are about the pastor's anointing, the more people are going to get mad at you; and the more you correct people from the pulpit, the more people are going to get mad at you. But that doesn't mean everyone will leave; that doesn't mean God won't fill your church to overflowing. People are looking to be disciplined. People are looking to be uplifted. People are looking for a man who will stand up and can't be bought; a man you can't put a price tag on.

How many of you would like to know the secrets of God? He reveals them to His true prophets, and then they speak them forth. These things will be edifying. Sometimes the messages will prick your heart, but they will still bring *life*. Just don't listen to a prophet who speaks doom all the time.

Let the prophets speak! Let them say what God is saying!

Secrets are going to be revealed in these last days through the prophets of the land, saith the Lord of hosts.

My pastors will not be bought with a price, but they will hear what I say to them in their study, and they will come out and teach what I say to teach.

Yea, listen to what the Spirit of the Lord is saying to the churches today! Listen to my anointed men. Listen to the prophets. Listen to the apostles. Listen to the pastors. And listen to the evangelists.

Many things are going to be said in these last days, and many will not heed the words that are spoken. They will fall and be destroyed, and they will come home to be with Me. They will be destroyed because they didn't listen and heed; because they wanted to go the world's way.

Give heed to what the Spirit of Grace and the Spirit of Truth is saying in these last days, saith the Lord of hosts; and you will surely prosper, and you will see the secret things that you need to know.

Many will not make it in these last days, but the ones who will listen to what the Spirit is saying to the churches will be successful.

There are some who have not prospered. You have said in your heart, "Well, I tried tithing, and it did not work. I didn't get blessed." Listen to the Spirit of the Lord. You saw a way to make money, but it doesn't work that way. I look upon the condition of your heart as you give unto Me. You must give because you want to give unto Me.

There will even come a time in some countries when you will not get a receipt and be able to claim your giving to the government. Then I'll find my true ones who will tithe unto Me, and I will bless them, and bless them, and bless them.

Prophecy delivered by Ed Dufresne

The prophets are coming! The prophets are coming! The prophets are coming! They will speak the secrets of God.

Surely the Lord God will do nothing but he revealeth his secret unto his servants the prophets.

Amos 3:7

Books by Ed Dufresne

There's A Healer In The House

Prophet: Friend Of God

Fresh Oil From Heaven

Praying God's Word

Faithfulness: The Road To Divine Promotion

How To Activate Miracles

How To Increase Your Anointing

The Believer Is A Winner

Without A Vision

You Can Stop Worry In Your Life

For a complete list of tapes and books by
Ed Dufresne, to be on his mailing list,
and to receive his free magazine, Jesus The Healer,
please write:

Ed Dufresne Ministries
P.O. Box 186
Temecula, CA 92593